COURTRIGHT MEMORIAL LIBRARY
OTTERBEIN COLLEGE
FOUNDED
1847
OF OHIO
WESTERVILLE

Presented by

Regnery Publishing, Inc.

Between the Alps
and a Hard Place

Between the Alps and a Hard Place

Switzerland in World War II and Moral Blackmail Today

ANGELO M. CODEVILLA

Since 1947
**REGNERY
PUBLISHING, INC.**
An Eagle Publishing Company • Washington, DC

Library of Congress Cataloging-in-Publication Data

    Codevilla, Angelo, 1943–
        Between the Alps and a hard place : Switzerland in World War II
    and moral blackmail today / Angelo M. Codevilla.
           p. cm.
        Includes bibliographical references and index.
        ISBN 0-89526-353-X
        1. World War, 1939–1945—Switzerland. 2. Switzerland—His-
tory—20th century. 3. Neutrality—Switzerland—History—20th century. I. Title

    D763.S9 C63 2000   00-040308

Published in the United States by
Regnery Publishing, Inc.
An Eagle Publishing Company
One Massachusetts Avenue, NW
Washington, DC 20001

Visit us at <www.regnery.com>.

Distributed to the trade by
National Book Network
4720-A Boston Way
Lanham, MD 20706

Printed on acid-free paper
Manufactured in the United States of America

10 9 8 7 6 5 4 3 2 1

Books are available in quantity for promotional or premium use. Write to
Director of Special Sales, Regnery Publishing, Inc., One Massachusetts
Avenue, NW, Washington, DC 20001, for information on discounts and
terms or call (202) 216-0600.

To my grandsons

Jeffrey
John
Matthew

Contents

Preface

THE SECOND WORLD WAR continues to teach a half century after its end because the greatest wars force people to deal with the full range of human experiences. It is especially useful to reflect on war's lessons during history's rare lengthy periods of peace because during such periods people tend so to misrepresent the harsh realities of war that they intellectually disarm themselves for future trials.

Switzerland's peculiar experience in World War II—managing to retain a degree of independence despite being surrounded by the Axis of Nazi Germany and Fascist Italy—teaches much about the complex meaning of deterrence, subversion, economic leverage, neutrality, the balance of power, and the balance between what a people want and what they can have. In short, the Swiss staved off Nazi occupation through military preparations, political ambivalence, and economic machinations—a combination of defiance and cooperation stemming less from calculation than from internal clashes. During the war, Allied economic warriors used to jest that the Swiss worked six days a week for the Axis, and on the seventh day prayed for an Allied victory. They could jest because they knew reality well.

But between 1995 and 1999, a publicity campaign orchestrated by the Clinton administration in conjunction with Edgar Bronfman, billionaire owner of a liquor and media empire, so caricatured the role of Switzerland in World War II that it led those unfamiliar with the realities of war to some dangerously wrong conclusions about how the world works. Bronfman, the largest family donor to the U.S. Democratic Party,[1] president and financier of the World Jewish Congress, used his formidable power to enlist the president of the United States, the chairman of the Senate Banking Committee, a network of state and local officials, a battery of lawyers, and the media to tell a startling tale: New discoveries showed that Switzerland had really been an ally of Nazi Germany, that the Swiss people shared culpability for the Holocaust, and that Swiss banks had stolen the assets of murdered Jews. Of course there was not a shred of new information in all of this. Bronfman nevertheless managed to convince Switzerland's two largest banks, which together make about $4 billion in profits per year in the United States, that they could do no more business in New York City unless they put a great deal of money at his disposal. So, on August 12, 1998, when these banks agreed to turn over $1.25 billion over three years to be administered chiefly by Mr. Bronfman's organization, the campaign came to an abrupt halt. The campaign, and Swiss actions in World War II, faded away. Too bad.

This campaign was significant in itself: A powerful private party induced officials of the United States, as well as the American legal system, to force foreigners who do business here to pay a huge bribe. Public officials served private interests without any legislative body taking a single vote, any executive official making a decision for which he might be held accountable, any court pronouncing a judgment or even ruling on the admissibility of evidence. This is another example of America's continuing movement away from the rule of law, as well as from a serious foreign policy.

That unseriousness consists in part of the franchising of foreign policy to domestic supporters of the Clinton administration—a policy constructed, as one commentator has put it, "by adding up the demands of domestic interest groups . . . whose discordant voices . . . are each allowed to dictate policy for a season."[2] The result, writes another wise observer, is that "[f]oreign governments have learned not to take seriously administration statements of its general policy goals and to take very seriously administration actions devoted to commercial and ethnic interests."[3] The fundamental reason why the American people permit such unseriousness is ignorance about the realities of international affairs in general as well as of the specific instances in which foreign policy is exercised.

The anti-Swiss campaign is as good an example as any. Reporters, editors, and the few who paid attention to the campaign failed to understand that they were being manipulated, in part because they were ignorant of history and of how nations deal with one another when they are serious. They should have known better than to accept uncritically a documentary showing munitions rolling off Swiss assembly lines while the voice professed shock, shock, that a self-proclaimed neutral country could have sold munitions to the Nazis. Anyone schooled in international affairs would have noted that the documentary never revealed that the Swiss were surrounded, and utterly bereft of the coal and oil they needed to sustain their army and to keep from starving and freezing. The Germans alone decided how much fuel the Swiss would get, at what price, and what they would accept in exchange. Adolf Hitler's Third Reich would not be satisfied with chocolate. What were the alternatives to selling precision instruments and munitions? How much could Switzerland shave from the amount that

Germany demanded? In the same documentary, Rabbi Israel Singer, the chief operating officer of the World Jewish Congress, called Switzerland's neutrality, and the fact that it did not declare war on Germany, an attempt at equidistance between evil and good. But anyone familiar with the balance of power in World War II would have known a Swiss war against Germany could only have produced millions more dead and enslaved— and unrestricted passage for military trains between Germany and Italy. Sophisticated audiences might also have asked what the anti–Swiss campaign meant to the purses and powers of its authors.

A sterile debate followed over whether the Swiss people had saved enough Jews. The answer to that question is "yes" if one compares the percentage of Jewish refugees in Switzerland's population (.5 percent) to the percentage of Jewish refugees in the population of the United States (.1 percent), and "no" if one compares the number of Jews that Switzerland sheltered with the number that it might have sheltered. Just as sterile was the debate about to what extent the Swiss bankers knew that the German gold they were converting into Swiss francs had been looted. This obscured the prior and more interesting questions: Why would the Swiss, who despised the Nazis viscerally, sell anything at all to that regime, what would they take in return, under what circumstances, and why?

This book explains why the Swiss corner of the vast tableau of World War II is interesting: The war forced a people whose degree of democracy and diversity is comparable only to America's to confront military, political, and economic challenges that are all too normal in international affairs. In 1940 Germany's unexpected military victories forced Switzerland to scrap longstanding military plans and adopt radically unpleasant new ones.

Especially interesting is how the new plans were built on a bru-
tally cold assessment of the country's few military assets. In the
political realm, Nazi Germany's encirclement of Switzerland, its
dominance of Europe, and its powerful subversive apparatus
almost succeeded in breaking the country's devotion to its
ideals—but failed. The struggle between various Swiss "hard-
liners" and "soft-liners" over the meaning of political prudence
shows how important it is to get that meaning right.

The economic relationship between Switzerland and Germany is one of history's finest illustrations of the principle that
the value of economic assets depends rather strictly on the balance of power. When Germany could have taken what it
wanted by force, the Swiss ceded much on credit. When victory
hung in the balance, Germany had to pay in gold. When the
Germans were losing, the Swiss took advantage of them. In
the end, Nazi gold became a liability.

The Axis's and Allies' dealings with Switzerland and other
"neutrals" in World War II also teach the classic but oft forgotten lesson that what one nation can ask of another depends
strictly on the extent to which it can help erase fear of others
while enhancing fear of itself.

This book ends with an examination of how Edgar Bronfman's harnessing just a bit of the power of the U.S. government fits into American foreign policy at the turn of the
twenty-first century. The book's aim is to lead Americans, after
fifty years without a world war, to ponder the seriousness of foreign policy in general and war in particular.

In the twenty-first century as ever, unseriousness about these
things has serious consequences. In March 1999 the United
States led the North Atlantic Treaty Organization (NATO) into
a war against Yugoslavia without really meaning to. Prior to

the war, discussion of objectives, military operations, and Yugoslav resistance was limited to terms that precluded proper consideration of the nature of the enemy and the enemy's objectives, what it would take to overcome them, and whether America or the "international coalition" was really willing to pay the price. Winston Churchill once warned his generals that in war one sometimes had to take the enemy into account. How much economic pressure on what part of the target would it take to accomplish what? What would the ground troops do? What sort of military operations would be required to impose one's will on the target? How much blood would it all cost?

Two weeks after the start of the 1999 Yugoslav war, a small article appeared in the *New York Times* titled "Conflict in the Balkans: Serbian Strategy."[4] It noted that Yugoslav troops were digging a sophisticated set of interlocking fortifications for their ground forces and air defenses in the country's mountainous terrain—which had been the essence of Yugoslavia's plan to impose maximum casualties on invading Soviet forces. The article also observed that the plan bore a striking resemblance to the strategy Switzerland employed to deter a German invasion during World War II by withdrawing of the bulk of its army into an "Alpine redoubt." Indeed, American and NATO leaders made it plain that they no more intended to sacrifice blood and treasure to dig the Yugoslavs out of their redoubt than the Germans had to dig the Swiss out of theirs a half century before the American high altitude bombing campaign turned out barely to have scratched the Serbian army.

By the time the West had become conscious of the fact that their conflict with Yugoslavia was a real war, of what the enemy was willing and able to do, and of what it would take to counter that—in other words, to take it seriously—the Yugoslavs had created "facts on the ground" and drawn the Americans into endless negotiations about them.

This book presents the lessons of the Swiss experience in World War II to an audience that has become accustomed to unrealistic images of war, and that risks learning war's deadly seriousness the hard way.

★ ★ ★ ★

Note on translations: Unless otherwise noted, all translations herein, including documents and publications in Switzerland's three languages—German, French, and Italian—are by this author. Although I use materials in all three, I prefer the two minority languages because German has never pleased my Latin tongue.

Angelo M. Codevilla
Dubois, Wyoming
June 2000

CHAPTER I

Pseudo Event
vs. Reality

*"When harsh accusations depart too far from the truth,
they leave bitter consequences."*

—Tacitus

BETWEEN JUNE 1995 AND AUGUST 12, 1998, a stream of
news reports, congressional hearings, and semi-official
committees of accountants and historians swirled around accusations that, contrary to what the world had thought for a half
century, Switzerland had really been an ally of Nazi Germany
in World War II. Worse, until now Switzerland had managed
to hide its Nazi profits, including money that Jews fleeing the
Holocaust had deposited in Swiss banks and that the banks
kept from their heirs, as well as gold torn from the rest of
Europe—indeed gold torn from the very teeth of gassed Jews.
Edgar Bronfman and his subordinates at the World Jewish
Congress demanded billions of dollars in reparations, to be
administered by organizations they controlled. Various parts of
the U.S. government, led by President Bill Clinton, supported
demands that the Swiss government pay up, lending substance
to the threat of U.S. economic sanctions on Switzerland. Significantly, U.S. officials were careful never to make the threats
officially.

The Swiss public reacted with resentment of everything American. Then on August 12, 1998, the two largest Swiss banks, Union Bank of Switzerland and Swiss Bank Corporation, plus Credit Suisse, agreed to pay $1.25 billion protection money to be allowed to continue to operate in the world's financial center, New York City. At that very moment, the fine points being debated by committees of historians, as well as the assessment by auditors under former U.S. Federal Reserve Chairman Paul Volcker of whether this or that unclaimed account might have belonged to Holocaust victims, became uninteresting. The winners dropped their righteous anger and got down to the business of scrapping over the take.

The term that best describes the anti-Swiss campaign of 1995–1999 is "pseudo event." A generation ago Librarian of Congress Daniel Boorstin coined it in his monumental book *The Image: A Guide to the Pseudo Event in America.*[1] Once upon a time, wrote Boorstin, real events had been reported because they had happened. Nowadays, pseudo events exist only to the extent that anyone succeeds in getting them reported. The artificial character of the controversy over Switzerland's newly discovered villainy becomes obvious the instant one realizes that absolutely no new information emerged. In 1996 then-Senator Alfonse D'Amato (R–NY), who did his best to spread the accusations, admitted as much, saying that even though the whole matter had been reviewed exhaustively a long time ago, it was new to him.[2] Alas, the past is full of things unknown to those who have not made the effort to learn them.

In fact, every last scrap of information in the charges, defenses, and countercharges had been placed in archives a half century ago after being thrashed out by the people who had experienced that part of the war. In short, the authors of the campaign resurrected parts of an old story to support judgments diametrically opposite to the judgments of the original protagonists.

To us, the degree of valor or villainy of the Swiss fifty years ago is less significant than that the Clinton administration and its allies bent the reality of a chapter of history to suit one of their party's constituents. Compromising America's standing in the world by franchising foreign policy to interest groups has become all too commonplace. More important, focusing attention on a historical event to serve current private interests dumbs down our understanding of how the world works. Both the attacks and the defenses focused on Swiss behavior rather than on the vital context of the war—looming inflation caused by Germany's extortion prices, Germany's nonpayment for industrial goods, the run on gold in the domestic Swiss market from around the globe, and so on. The controversy has thus detracted rather than contributed to our understanding of the art of policy-making under duress.

The experience of Switzerland, a free-market democracy trapped for four years between the Alps and the Nazis, is full of lessons about mixing military deterrence with economic incentives, and balancing the internal politics of a diverse country with the international balance of power. The Swiss experience also drives home the age-old lesson that the capacity of any country to influence another is proportionate to its capacity to harm or to protect the other. American statesmen in World War II knew these lessons. But their grandchildren who play with images are largely ignorant of them.

A Pseudo Event

The least important lessons concern the anti–Swiss campaign itself. These are largely about the state of American politics at the end of the twentieth century. In short, the only real event was that another coalition of powerful Americans had mounted another campaign using the power and prestige of the United States government to funnel money into its own hands.

A shrewd observer could see that the campaign against Switzerland was a pseudo event because those who waged it did not really mean what they said. Some, including U.S. officials, spoke as if the Swiss people, with whom the United States had always been friendly, had really been enemies all along. They broadly hinted at economic reprisals unless the Swiss paid a heavy sum—not to the U.S. Treasury, on behalf of the public, but to certain *private* organizations. But, if the charges of a covert alliance with the Nazis were true, the remedy—paying to the World Jewish Congress and other private organizations a fraction of one percent of Switzerland's yearly gross domestic product (GDP)—surely was too light. If Switzerland had *really* been an accomplice to some of this century's worst crimes, if we had *really* just found out that the Swiss had been in on Hitler's schemes, the proper course of action would have been to treat Switzerland as a treacherous enemy. But no one introduced a bill in Congress to these ends. Nor did the U.S. government make *or even formally study* making such a serious charge. Nor did any department of government even consider renouncing the 1946 U.S.–Swiss agreement that settled the claims arising out of World War II, much less did any department consider economic warfare against Switzerland.

This, then, was just another instance of the semi-official use of American power to transfer cash from not-so-favored parties to powerful officials' favored private constituents, who then recycle some of the money back to the officials who made it all possible. A basic feature of pseudo events is that they serve the interests of their creators. Edgar Bronfman's World Jewish Congress, the principal creator of the campaign outside of government, was also among its beneficiaries. As for President Clinton and Senator D'Amato, Edgar Bronfman paid them in advance with major political contributions. In sum, contemporary American politicians play with humanitarian and moral outrage as they do with other deadly tools of statecraft.

On April 23, 1996, Senator D'Amato opened a hearing of the U.S. Senate Banking Committee he chaired, claiming, "We have in our possession recently declassified documents that shed new light" on Switzerland's role in World War II.[3] D'Amato claimed that the money deposited in Swiss banks in the 1930s by Jews like the father of one of his constituents, Greta Beer, amounted to "[h]undreds of millions of dollars of assets . . . monies under the direction of the Nazis being hidden away in Switzerland, we'll get to that."[4] The only evidence for this nonsensical statement was a hearsay report from 1945 that cited someone saying that he had deposited $28 million in a Swiss bank. The Swiss government claimed that only $32 million in unclaimed assets remained in major banks in 1996.

The only documentation D'Amato cited was an article in the *Wall Street Journal* that had broken no new ground but rather had reported charges the World Jewish Congress had made against Switzerland.[5] The emotional component at the hearing came from the elderly Mrs. Beer, who said her father had told her before the war that he had deposited a lot of money in a Swiss bank. She didn't know how much or in which bank, much less had she ever seen a passbook or an account number. Pitifully, she recounted that after the war, she and her mother had gone from bank to bank, and that no bank had come up with any money.[6] What *monsters*, asked D'Amato, would oppose justice for a sweet old lady like Mrs. Beer? (And how shameful should someone note that D'Amato had proved nothing.) Shame too on the bank employees who refused to hand money to a stranger walking up to the window with a story about a dead depositor.

Then came the threat, and it involved more money than the combined total of what families such as the Beers ever possessed. Edgar Bronfman testified that

> . . . the documents uncovered by your committee and by others working elsewhere demonstrate that during the Nazi era the Swiss were far from neutral. Their assistance to the Nazi war machine through the clandestine conversion of looted gold into Swiss francs enabled the Germans to buy fuel and other raw materials they needed to prolong the war. Some estimates in testimony before the U.S. Senate hearings following the war suggest the costs may have been staggering in the lives of American soldiers, Allied soldiers, Jews, and other civilians across the continent.

Having transformed suggestions into facts and accusations into proof, Bronfman asserted: "I speak to you today on behalf of the Jewish people. With reverence, I also speak to you on behalf of the six million who cannot speak for themselves."[7] Then, having taken onto himself all that power and moral authority, Bronfman took on the right to dispose of what he called the rightful patrimony of the victims of Nazism. D'Amato spoke of "hundreds of millions" of dollars, while Bronfman spoke of "billions." The money, said Bronfman, would go to survivors of the Holocaust, as well as to individuals and institutions, museums and writers who would keep alive the memory of the Holocaust. The survivors were few and dwindling, while the latter categories would become long-term political supporters of those who would provide their livelihoods with Swiss money.

Note that at this point Bronfman and D'Amato intended the money to come from the Swiss government—that is, from Swiss taxpayers. Why should the Swiss people have paid any attention to these demands, much less felt the need to comply? Because behind the demands was the threatening insistence of the Clinton administration. The threat was first delivered by Ambassador Stuart Eizenstat, U.S. special envoy for property claims in Central and Eastern Europe, U.S. undersecretary of commerce, and a friend of President Clinton.

Eizenstat reported to the Senate that his purpose was to achieve openness in reporting about unclaimed accounts in Swiss banks, to make sure that heirs got what was properly due them and that heirless assets were distributed to poor elderly Jews in Eastern Europe. Who could object? But Eizenstat also reported that his practical job was to add the authority of the U.S. government to the claims of Mr. Bronfman's organization, through "government to government conversations and facilitation with international and local organizations."[8] The practical meaning was that, until Bronfman *et al.* were happy with Switzerland, the U.S. government wouldn't be happy either. D'Amato underlined this as he concluded Eizenstat's testimony: "I have every confidence that we will have a full court press led by you on behalf of the Administration." This full court press included U.S. Ambassador to Bern Madeleine Kunin's countless interventions as well as a speech to the Swiss parliament by Secretary of State Madeleine Albright.

Note that Ambassador Eizenstat's formal job description—to promote "the nondiscriminatory, transparent, and just resolution of claims arising out of properties confiscated during and after the Second World War by the Nazis and their sympathizers or by the communist governments in Central and Eastern Europe"—did not include Switzerland at all. Nevertheless, his pressuring of the Swiss included commissioning a voluminous U.S. government report that bears his name and served as the basis for campaigns against Switzerland and other Western European countries.

The preface to the Eizenstat report asks, "Why the sudden surge of interest in these tragic events of four decades ago?" And it answers: "[T]he most compelling reason is the extraordinary leadership and vision of a few people who have put this issue on the world's agenda: . . . Edgar Bronfman, Israel Singer, . . . Senator Alfonse D'Amato of New York, and President Bill Clinton. . . ."[9] The report also leaves no doubt that these extraordinary leaders were adopting judgments that had been aired and rejected during the Roosevelt and Truman administrations. Rather than discovering new facts, the Eizenstat report reversed the values placed on old facts by Americans who had actually fought and defeated Nazi Germany. In presenting his report, Eizenstat said, "Our task is to complete the unfinished business of the twentieth century's most traumatic and tragic events," while the report's principal drafter, William Slany, spoke frankly of reversing the actions of a previous generation, of "doing things now that couldn't be done then."

According to the report, "As late as the end of 1944 Secretary of State E.R. Stettinius, Jr., and his State Department colleagues concluded that, on balance, Switzerland's neutrality had been more a positive than a negative for the Allies during the War."[10]

But, the report notes, there were people in the U.S. government, primarily in Henry Morgenthau's Treasury Department and in the Office of Strategic Services (OSS), who did not think so well of the Swiss. Indeed there were. The report, however, does not mention that these people lost policy arguments within the U.S. government on the merits (for example, the Morgenthau Plan to pastoralize Germany) as well as because they tended to follow the Soviet line. Nor does it ever explain why the anti-Swiss views should be accorded greater credence than the pro-Swiss views. Rather, the report simply piles accusation upon accusation, and, in short, blames the presidents and secretaries of state of the time for discounting the anti-Swiss claims: "The U.S. government . . . over the objections of the Treasury Department, decided not to pursue sanctions."[11] The implication was that this decision had been incorrect, and that the U.S. government now had grounds, if not an obligation, to act otherwise.

Senator D'Amato aptly summed up the effect of this litany by faulting the "moral fortitude" of the people who ran America at the time because they "ran out on our obligation" by not treating Switzerland as a hostile power. As a result, D'Amato said he was ashamed of being an American. Strong stuff. But not serious.

Had the report and the campaign attempted to remake the image of Switzerland in America rather than provide a pretext for extortion they would have had a big job. Americans have traditionally had a most favorable image of the Swiss. On the lowest level, the Swiss were seen as Alpine yodelers who make fine chocolate, watches, and camping knives.

The bible of the middlebrow, *National Geographic*, has offered moving descriptions of how the International Committee of the

Red Cross, organized in Switzerland by the Swiss, has tempered the horrors of war and ministered to the victims of disaster.[12] Europe and the world, says the *Geographic*, are lucky that the roof of the old continent is occupied by such a multiethnic, multireligious nation, dedicated to peace within itself and with its neighbors. International institutions that seek the peace of the world have made their headquarters in Switzerland, which is seen as a haven for the oppressed. Even Senator Barbara Boxer (D-CA), a staunch Clinton supporter and backer of the accusations, began her statement to D'Amato's committee by stating this standard view: "[M]y memory as a child is that Switzerland really acted as a haven for many Jews who escaped. I had a cousin there who [*sic*] I visited, and he and his wife actually used Switzerland as a base from which they actually got many Jews out of Germany and other parts of Europe. So it is ironic that we've run into this situation."[13] D'Amato followed suit by confessing that he too had shared the common herd's ignorance of Swiss villainy, and wondered what sort of base reasons might have led so many to hide it for so long.

The pro-Swiss, right-wing conspiracy at the highest levels of culture must have been vast indeed. Prior to 1995 hardly a harsh word about the Swiss could be found in serious literature. In 1512 Niccolò Machiavelli, from whose pen praise did not flow easily, described the Swiss as "most armed and most free"—a people who knew the fundamentals of statecraft and used them to guard their sober way of life.[14] Stanford historian James Murray Luck and CUNY professor Rolf Kieser are among the many authors who spread the image of Switzerland as America's "sister republic," a place where most issues are decided at the local level by direct popular vote, and where even national-level decisions are most often made by referendum.[15]

Neither federalism nor democracy could exist, never mind in such straight doses, if the population were not unusually habituated to tolerance and the practice of civic virtues. Foremost among these is universal military service.

As regards World War II, the most authoritative judgment on Switzerland came from Winston Churchill, whose personal commitment to decent government might well have surpassed even that of Bill Clinton, and whose knowledge of Nazi machinations must at least have matched that of Alfonse D'Amato. Churchill wrote:

> I put this down for the record. Of all the neutrals, Switzerland has the greatest right to distinction. She has been the sole international force linking the hideously sundered nations and ourselves. What does it matter if she has not been able to give us commercial advantages we desire or has given too many to the Germans to keep herself alive? She has been a democratic state standing for freedom in self-defense among her mountains, and in thought, in spite of race, largely on our side.[16]

One can only wonder whether Clinton and Eizenstat, confronting live Nazis at the height of their power rather than their discredited memory, would have dealt with them with any less deference than they showed to the Soviet Union when it had the wind in its sails.[17] In fact, when Hitler was riding high only one European or American statesman ever refused a chance to pay his respects to him. That man was Winston Churchill. But if Clinton, D'Amato, and Eizenstat were correct about Switzerland, does Churchill's expression of solidarity with the Swiss mean that he was ill informed or insufficiently anti-Nazi?[18] As for

Presidents Roosevelt and Truman and their secretaries of state, who treated Switzerland as a friend in straitened circumstances rather than as a Nazi ally, were they dupes too?

Those actually in charge of running the economic war against the Axis powers long ago explained why the people responsible for Allied foreign policy treated Switzerland as they did. In 1946 David L. Gordon and Royden Dangerfield wrote how the U.S. government's "Blockade Division, Foreign Economic Administration," which they had headed, had pressured neutral countries to reduce economic activity with the Axis and to contribute to the Allied war effort. Switzerland, they wrote, had been judged a special case because it was totally surrounded. Hence, Allied economic warriors allowed Switzerland to trade on the world market five times as much "enemy content" as other neutral countries were permitted. As for who was on whose side, these men wrote:

> The great majority of Swiss and Swedes unquestionably hoped the Allies would win. But the Allies did not threaten invasion while the Nazis did. So until an Allied victory appeared certain and imminent both Sweden and Switzerland deviated from strict neutrality only in one direction, in favor of Germany. They gave way reluctantly, yielding inch by inch, stalling as long as possible, and taking advantage of every bargaining point which promised to give them room for maneuver—but they still gave way. They did fight stubbornly, however, to preserve contact with the Allied world. . . . Thus they remained little islands of peace and relative plenty in the enslaved and beleaguered continent.[19]

In his preface to their book *The Hidden Weapon*, Thomas K. Finletter, who served as special assistant to Secretary of State E. R. Stettinius, Jr., and was a close confidant of Franklin Roosevelt, tells readers that Gordon and Dangerfield and their Blockade Division had admirably carried out the victorious policy of the administration.

On what bases then does the Eizenstat report contradict such judgments? In fact, *the report does not even attempt to show why Churchill, Roosevelt, Stettinius, or America's economic warriors were wrong*—and therefore forfeits intellectual respectability. But when you have power and social standing, who needs respectability?

The Eizenstat report also takes up the *chevaux de bataille* that extreme leftists within Switzerland had been trying to ride ever since the war. Switzerland is a very conservative country. Women didn't get the vote in national elections until 1971. Pet proposals of intellectuals on the extreme left, such as abolition of universal military service, regularly get trounced in referenda. The Swiss Socialist Party threw out its extreme leftist minority midway through World War II. Ever since, these marginalized leftist intellectuals have tried to delegitimize their country's social order by tarring it with nothing less than guilt for collaborating with the Holocaust. The *New York Times Magazine* summed it all up with a quote from Swiss novelist and notorious extremist Adolf Muschg: "Auschwitz was also in Switzerland."[20] Perhaps to show its disregard for conventional notions of truth, the *Times* did not point out that this statement was literally false, and that literal falsehoods are to be found throughout that set of accusations. Read the magazine *Une Suisse Sans Armée*, a publication of the Swiss far left, and see with what pride, for over a half century, all the themes of the Clinton administration's campaign have been part of extreme leftist pro-paganda: Switzerland's sociopolitical system shares responsibility for the murder of Europe's Jews.[21] Nevertheless all this was sufficient for the Clinton administration.

According to the Clinton administration, then, people like Winston Churchill, Franklin Roosevelt, and Harry Truman, nearly all historians, the flood of journalists and ordinary people who have dealt with Switzerland over the past half century—all are dupes at best and at worst soft on Nazism.

Now, to take reality seriously, what insights into the logic of international affairs did the successes and shortcomings of the Swiss in World War II provide?

Military Deterrence

Prior to 1940 the Swiss military publicly relied on its well-advertised capacity to muster in arms over 10 percent of the population in well-prepared border positions, to defend its internationally guaranteed neutrality against all comers. But in reality, since the rise of nation-states the military safety of tiny Switzerland has depended on the willingness of a neighboring power to rush its army into Switzerland to help block another neighboring power from using Switzerland for its own ends. Thus in World War I the Swiss held off the Germans by the prospect that they would call in the French, and held off the French by the prospect that they would call in the Germans. When World War II began, the Swiss feared Germany exclusively. But they hoped that France, and even Italy, would know enough and be potent enough to help safeguard their own Swiss flanks. When France fell and Italy joined Germany, Switzerland was quite unexpectedly thrown back on its own military resources.

At most these military resources could make Germany's price of conquest too heavy to pay. And that depended on the extent to which Switzerland could maximize the value of its three military assets: Alpine terrain, the Gotthard and Simplon tunnels, and the Swiss soldier's historic bloody-mindedness. But exploiting Alpine terrain to the maximum essentially meant sacrificing half the country and more than two-thirds of the population. Holding hostage the tunnels and the country's infrastructure meant destroying the Swiss people's livelihood. Making the most of the Swiss soldier's penchant to fight to the death meant firing up the population's martial spirit, which many influential Swiss believed was already provoking Germany.

On various occasions Germany's *Wehrmacht* estimated that defeating the Swiss army would take three to six days—about as long as it had taken to defeat the Belgian army—and require nine to twelve divisions, including four armored.[22] The reason for this confidence was that the Swiss army had not changed since World War I. A modern force could easily negate its trenches and machine guns spread out along the northern plateau. But the German High Command added one qualification: The Swiss army must not be allowed to retreat in good order southward into the Alps. Once ensconced in the mountain valleys, the Swiss would be nearly impossible to dig out.

For its part, the Swiss army reached the same conclusions, which led it to withdraw the bulk of its forces from the northern plateau into the southern Alpine valleys. While the military logic of this national redoubt was self-evident, its political logic was much less so. After all, redeploying meant abandoning at least two-thirds of the population, including the families of the soldiers, to Nazi occupation. On the other hand, if the army

remained deployed on the plateau it would be defeated anyway, and the whole country occupied. But while no Swiss
wanted to leave the country's major cities open to occupation,
no German wanted to see the Swiss army holed up in the Alps,
cutting off the vital Simplon and Gotthard tunnels to the
Mediterranean and threatening guerrilla warfare. Thus the
Swiss adopted a military strategy that threatened to accept
grievous losses in order to deter the enemy. But of course most
deterrence strategies aim to avoid being put to the ultimate
test. Military deterrence is usually a shield for and an adjunct
to other policies that mean to avoid war. This was the case in
Switzerland.

The Political Home Front

What policies—political, economic, military—would suit a
democratic, pluralistic country surrounded by enemies dispos-
ing of thirty times its manpower and resources? It would have
been strange indeed if the answer had not aroused hot dispute.
The Swiss people never doubted that Nazi Germany was the
enemy. But how could their government resist the pressure of
those emboldened to seek profit from what appeared to be Germany's inevitable victory? The Swiss also had some Communists who at first backed Hitler and then, after the Nazis invaded
the Soviet Union, made trouble. They too had greedy businessmen and weak politicians. Officially and unofficially, the
Swiss had to learn to speak softly to and about Germany, since
Switzerland's stick was small. Yet how can a people keep its spir-
its up while biting its tongue? How can a nation reaffirm principles of individual and economic freedom when circumstances
demand that it empower economic planners and even institute
compulsory labor to raise food?

In 1940 Germany's military victories dazzled much of the world into moral defeat. Since power is something around which human beings instinctively bend, the peoples of continental Europe vied to adjust to the New World Order. Throughout the world (not least in Washington, D.C.) Charles de Gaulle's call to honor and resistance was widely deemed foolish. The Soviet Union and the progressive Western leaders who followed it opposed resisting Nazi Germany in thought, word, or deed. In America Franklin Roosevelt described Hitler's New Europe with minced words, in part because some of his major constituents, such as Joseph Kennedy, were sympathetic to it, while other Roosevelt supporters took their bearings from Hitler's ally, Stalin. From behind the English Channel Winston Churchill roared defiance like the lion he was. Yet this throwback to a nobler age barely managed to dominate an Establishment rotten with pro-Nazis.

In Switzerland, surrounded and multiethnic, whose every aspect ran counter to every precept of Hitler's New Europe, whose press daily insulted Hitler in his own language, where the full panoply of Nazi subversion was at work, the task of maintaining coherence, of steering the ship of state between the twin shoals of capitulation and recklessness, was inherently difficult. During the Cold War, the world developed the word "Finlandization" to describe the lot of a small, free people cut off from the community of free peoples and forced to come to terms with a neighboring totalitarian superpower. Wartime Switzerland, however, managed to retain a greater degree of independence than did Finland.

The outcome of the struggle for the Swiss home front was in doubt only during the summer of 1940. While diplomats and industrialists were conciliating the Germans, the Swiss army's commander in chief, Henri Guisan, was rallying the troops and forcing the politicians' choices. One of Guisan's instruments, the organization Army and Hearth, spread determination through society's capillaries. Though Swiss President Marcel Pilet Golaz was inclined to conciliate, he responded to public opinion, which was following the army, and agreed to banish the enemy's partisans from the political process. The Swiss reaffirmed their own and the enemy's identity by arresting and executing substantial numbers of Swiss citizens who spied for Germany. Fortunately, as Germany's victory became more doubtful after 1942, fighting Nazi subversion became easier.

As a lifeboat in the midst of shipwrecks, Switzerland was a magnet for all kinds of refugees. When its minister of justice and police declared in 1942 that "the lifeboat is full," Switzerland, a country of 4 million, already had about 80,000 refugees. By the end of the war that number had risen to some 300,000. Of these approximately 20,000 were Jews, the number of Jewish refugees amounting to one-half of 1 percent of Switzerland's population. Proportionately, this was five times as many Jewish refugees as the United States admitted.

The one peculiar aspect of Switzerland's behavior toward refugees—namely, the contrast between what the central government prescribed and what actually happened—is due to Switzerland's unique decentralized structure. In essence, the federal government set restrictive rules on the inflow of refugees, cantonal governments applied them differently, local governments bent them, and private organizations and individuals (presumably including Senator Barbara Boxer's relatives) often ignored them, especially when facing the human consequences of deporting such vulnerable human beings. That is why the lifeboat continued to fill, especially after the man nominally in charge of it declared it full.

The prototypical case occurred in Zurich in 1942. A young Belgian Jewish couple who had escaped into Switzerland spent the night in the city's Jewish cemetery. With the greatest courtesy, local policemen took them to the police station and contacted the federal authorities, who, the police believed, would provide for the couple. When the federals instead deported the young couple, individuals and local authorities in Zurich began to hide refugees. Ordinary citizens in border areas did the same; they were shocked at the pitiful sight of refugees turned back by border guards. Unsurprisingly, as the fortunes of war shifted against the Axis, more refugees got in. The balance of power did not determine behavior, but it counted for a lot.

The Balance of Power

Were the Swiss then just weathervanes, blowing with the prevailing winds? The classics of international affairs teach that even great nations, like great sailing ships, must live by the balance of the wind's power. The great texts of statesmanship, including Thucydides' *Peloponnesian War* and Machiavelli's *Discourses*, treat the decision whether, or how, to intervene in conflicts as one of the weightiest and most complex that statesmen ever have to make. They ask: Which side is likeliest to hurt us if we do not join it? How well can we defend ourselves against the displeasure of everyone who has a stake in the conflict? George Washington and Alexander Hamilton, who were alert to such considerations, would have chuckled at Rabbi Israel Singer's charge that by remaining neutral in World War II Switzerland had chosen an equidistant position in a fight between good and evil.

Recall that America's first major decision in international affairs was whether to join revolutionary France, which had helped America win independence in its war against England. American public opinion was pro-French and anti-British. Washington and Hamilton, however, pointed out that none of this made up for the fact that American ships and troops could affect neither the character of the French Revolution nor the war's outcome. By joining the war, America would not help France but only harm itself.[23] Though the notion of equidistance never occurred to them, Washington and Hamilton sought to trade with both sides. England and France respected America's neutrality only to the tiny extent that American forces could enforce it. Since it turned out that England could hurt America more than France could, America was forced to tilt toward England. America nevertheless persisted in trying to force England to respect its neutrality. The consequence was the War of 1812.

Equidistance, then, was no more part of the Swiss notion of neutrality in World War II than it had been of early American neutrality. True, early Americans valued neutrality chiefly because of a temporary weakness, while the Swiss long ago recognized that they would always be weaker than their neighbors. Yet among true statesmen, neutrality and war are always means to ends, never ends in themselves. After World War I Switzerland had largely abandoned neutrality when it joined the League of Nations, which promised universal security. But when Hitler's occupation of the Rhineland and his *Anschluss* of Austria proved the league a cruel joke, Switzerland retreated into neutrality once again, even as its public opinion was becoming more anti-German than ever. In the months leading up to the outbreak of war, the Swiss army—blatantly violating neutrality—was secretly planning joint operations with the French army. France was Switzerland's hope. When that collapsed, Swiss neutrality became a plea to Germany. That plea was backed by an army that understood its own weakness, by an economy that was worth more alive than dead, and by a political system that managed to limit the influence of its enemies. Meanwhile, surrounded Switzerland hoped Germany would lose the war.

Historically, neutrals are pressured by both sets of belligerents. In World War II Switzerland was in the center of two concentric blockades. The outer blockade, run by the Allies, restricted world commerce to and from Switzerland on the reasonable ground that the Germans could pressure the Swiss to share their commerce. The inner blockade, run by the Germans, restricted Swiss exports to the Allies on the reasonable ground that Swiss products could help the Allies. To increase the pressure, Germany also restricted Swiss imports of fuel and food. The result of these blockades was that the Swiss had to obtain agreements from both the Axis and the Allies for every pound of cargo that entered or left the country. This meant that the Axis and Allies had to bargain with one another through Swiss intermediaries. They both knew the pressures that the other was putting on the Swiss. The total transparency of the compromises that resulted renders ludicrous today's claims that their secrets are just now being discovered. Nevertheless, because the daily business of economic warfare consisted of squeezing the enemy largely by squeezing the neutrals, the Germans retaliated for Swiss concessions to the Allies, and the Allies for Swiss concessions to the Germans.

Both sides realized that, especially in the case of Switzerland, it was best not to squeeze too hard. Both sides relied on Switzerland to look after their prisoners of war. Both used it as a mailbox to communicate with one another, and as a base for espionage on one another. Tacitly, the Allies allowed the Germans some access to world goods through Switzerland. The Allies openly purchased through Switzerland the one industrial product that Germany produced better than anyone else—namely, glass eyes.

Economic Deterrence

When a fortress is surrounded, it can usually be taken by economic strangulation. The German demands on Switzerland were mainly economic. Since Switzerland depended on foreign trade for over half its food, nearly all its fuel, the whole wherewithal of its industrial economy, and depended entirely on German permission to import anything at all, the Germans could obtain many (but not all) of the benefits of occupation without its inconveniences. Whenever the Swiss would balk too hard at some demand, the Germans would cut off coal shipments or block delivery of wheat the Swiss had purchased in Argentina. On the other hand, the Swiss franc's status as the world's only remaining freely convertible major currency—a currency that all belligerents needed for their relations with the world's neutrals—gave Switzerland considerable economic leverage over the Axis. The economic relationship between the two countries changed as the course of the war changed.

Under such conditions, the question is not whether to give in to the besieger's demands, but how much. The strategy of the besieged must be to maintain as much control as possible over the slippery process of concession. The tactics include maintaining as much as possible the pretense that the economic relationship is businesslike and not a reflection of the balance of power. Success is measured by the incentives given to the enemy to postpone military operations, the time gained during which the balance of power might shift, and how well damage to the economy is limited. Rarely can a besieged fortress increase the importance of its military deterrent. Switzerland managed this difficult feat through its economic relationship with its besieger. By the end of the war Switzerland was stronger than in 1940, having diverted to its own military some of the resources that Germany had allowed through the blockade.

The combination of Switzerland's military and economic deterrents in fact managed to stave off attack until Germany itself was overwhelmed. For this the Swiss paid an economic price, perhaps high, perhaps low. But indisputably the price, and the character of the economic relationship, varied during the course of the war along with the changing balance of power. The stranglehold on fuel and food remained constant until 1945. However, as German victory became questionable and then unlikely, as Germany's capacity to spare troops to overcome Switzerland's military deterrent decreased, Germany's power to compel deliveries on the basis of new credits disappeared. The power of the Swiss franc, which during the first stages of the war had limited damage to the economy, by the end was serving to repair some of that damage.

In war, all international economic relationships depend on the balance of power. Neither Nazi Germany nor the Soviet Union needed money to obtain many goods and services from their own peoples or from occupied countries. Force sufficed. To get unskilled labor from those they controlled, the Nazis set up slave labor camps. None of the inmates profited. Getting more complex goods and services from occupied countries involved somewhat subtler forms of enslavement, such as price-

and wage-controls. Very few French or Dutch got more than a pittance for backing such schemes.

To get what they wanted from Sweden, which they almost surrounded, and from Switzerland, which they surrounded completely, the Nazis relied on a combination of economic constraint—namely, rationing food and fuel at high prices—and of incentives backed by threats of violence. Nevertheless, some Swedes involved in selling iron ore, and some Swiss involved in selling machine tools and weapons to Germany—on credit supplied under duress by their countries' banks—made money. By contrast, to get what they wanted from Spain and Portugal, which they could threaten only a little, the Nazis had to pay top prices often in competition with Allied counterpurchases. Hence Spanish and Portuguese involved in the sale of tungsten made enormous amounts of money.

Whereas Sweden or Switzerland might feel obliged to deliver goods to Germany on bad credit, Spain, Portugal, and Turkey would not deliver tungsten and chrome to Germany for Reichsmarks, whose value they doubted. Nor would they sell for gold because, beginning in 1942, these countries began to doubt that Germany could harm them and, fearing the Allies, heeded their warnings against accepting German gold. In 1942–1943 the Allies objected less if the neutrals accepted Swiss francs. That is why Germany used the gold it had before the war and the gold it stole during the war to buy about 1.3 billion Swiss francs. Germany used these francs to buy Spanish, Portuguese, and other goods, either directly or with escudos or pesetas bought on the free Swiss currency market. Then the central banks of Spain, Portugal, Sweden, and so forth, quickly converted both francs and local currencies into gold on Switzerland's free gold market. Thus these countries wound up owning large amounts of gold from Germany without violating the Allies' warning too blatantly. In other words, much of the gold that Germany had or stole passed through Swiss hands but ended up in the accounts of other neutrals that supplied large amounts of tangible goods. All of this was entirely transparent.

The Swiss were not in a political, military, or economic position to refuse the transactions. In those hinge years, the Allies' main means of cutting down the flow of tungsten, chrome, and iron ore to Germany was to offer the neutrals Swiss francs, which they also bought for gold. But by 1944 the Allies' prospects of victory had become real enough that they did not need money of any kind to influence the neutrals. Their power was better currency than any money, or even gold. Conversely, because Germany's relative power had declined, it could offer no currency attractive enough to overcome Spain's and Portugal's reluctance to displease the Allies. By then the Turks had declared war on Germany to please the Allies. In sum, all of these transactions occurred at the price they did, in the shape they did, when they did, because the balance of power was what it was.

The Allies, too, needed gold-convertible Swiss francs, because the dollar and sterling's postwar value were uncertain, because other currencies were even less acceptable, and because settling international accounts by transporting gold overseas was too risky and cumbersome. So they used gold to buy about 2.2 billion Swiss francs. But when the Swiss National Bank made these francs available, American and British authorities paid the gold into accounts at the New York Federal Reserve Bank—frozen, along with the bulk of the prewar gold that Switzerland had deposited in New York for safekeeping.

Switzerland could make no use of any of it to support the value of the franc at home. Moreover, beginning in 1943, Allied economic demands on Switzerland were backed by the threat to appropriate all or part of this gold unless their demands were satisfied.

To understand why and how the value of currencies fluctuates with the balance of power, one must realize that, contrary to the popular misconception that money makes power, in fact power gives money whatever value it has.[24] If Germany had won the war, all the gold in Europe, regardless of country, bank, or account, would have been at its disposal, and all of Germany's debts would have been uncollectible. But as Germany was losing total war totally, it became clear that its financial assets would be taken totally in (minimal) compensation for German debts incurred and German damages done. There were more claims against Germany than German assets could possibly satisfy. The gold that Germany had stolen from the central banks and private parties of occupied countries had been liquidated to pay more or less willing suppliers for goods that were ground to dust in the war. When it became clear that Germany would be defeated, German assets in Reichsmarks or in stocks in Germany's domestic companies became worthless. Only the assets of German companies abroad, or in foreign accounts in foreign currencies, had any value. But since Germany had lost all power, those values effectively belonged to the countries where they were located. All of the countries where German assets existed—including the United States and Britain, but also the neutral countries—seized the assets, against their own much larger claims.

Given the disproportion between claims and assets to satisfy them, an unhappy set of international negotiations ensued. The saddest part was that the countries that had lost the most—pre-eminently Poland—had the least power over German assets. Most disadvantaged of all were the millions of individuals throughout Europe who had spent the war years working hard for submarginal livelihoods. Nearly all Europeans had been stripped of their lives' savings. The Germans had confiscated all private gold. People were understandably eager to believe that all that vanished wealth must be hidden away somewhere, and that it could be restored if someone would only crack open the vaults. But it really was gone.

The victorious Allies toyed with the idea of combing German assets out of neutral countries—though not out of their own—and dedicating the money to relieve a suffering continent. But the neutrals objected on the reasonable ground that they too had been victims of German or Soviet power. All the neutrals had legitimate claims against which to apply German assets that happened to be within their borders. Comparatively, Switzerland had lost less than, say, Belgium, but more than, say, Portugal. Switzerland, however, had power over a disproportionate chunk of German assets. So Allied negotiators brought greatest pressure on Switzerland. In the end, all sides made token payments to relieve Europe's misery, and agreed that the way to recovery lay not in fighting over small leftovers but in building anew.

Lessons

Attempts to revise tragedy usually end up as farce. The notion that the major chunks of Europe's wealth that disappeared during Hitler's war must still exist, hidden away in Swiss banks by the "Gnomes of Zurich," has been a staple of conspiracy theories for a half century. Through most of this period it remained confined to the fever swamps of believers in the omnipotence of money, who see profiteers behind every disaster. Then in the 1980s what one might call the Oliver Stone view of history-as-conspiracy became fashionable among academics. In the universities, prestigious people also touted the notion that history could mean anything one wanted. In the ranks of society, growing ignorance predisposed audiences to accept anything. During the 1990s, as U.S. foreign policy was being franchised to interest groups, the public did not blink at a campaign to build a pseudo-historical base for blackmailing Switzerland to give up allegedly bloodstained billions.

The details of this campaign are the least important part of this book. More important are the lessons to be drawn about the role of the balance of power in relations between belligerents and countries in various stages of neutrality and engagement, as well as the lessons to be drawn about the economic power of tyrants.

CHAPTER 2

Military

*"The race is not necessarily to the swift, nor the battle
to the strong."*

—Proverb

DURING WORLD WAR II the Swiss army deterred an Axis war
machine thirty times its strength from invading its home-
land. This contains lessons for strong and weak states alike. History
is full of examples of weaker nations that survive encounters
with the stronger, and sometimes prevail. American history
reminds us that thirteen weak colonies defeated the mighty
British Empire, that America at the height of its power was
defeated by tiny Vietnam, and that little Serbia stood off the
whole NATO alliance. By definition, the strong can crush the
weak. But in real life there are countless reasons why the strong
may commit only a portion of their strength. If then the weak
use all of theirs well, the actual balance of power in a specific
circumstance may sometimes give the weak a precarious edge. If
both the weak and the strong judiciously work the margins of
the balance of power, both may get what circumstances dictate
at any given time.

When a large, powerful country intends to rule a smaller,
weaker one, it must measure what resistance it may meet and
what it is willing to do to overcome that resistance. The smaller
target, for its part, must ask what combination of military

deterrence and concession will avoid the worst. Machiavelli wrote: "Princes who are set upon by forces much greater than their own can make no greater error than to refuse terms of settlement, especially when they are offered. Because never will an offer be so low as not to contain some element of good for those who accept them. And these shall be part of their victory."[1]

Two-and-a-half millennia ago, a dialogue of the deaf took place between the Athenians who were besieging the small Greek city of Melos with overwhelming forces, and the Melian rulers. The Melians demanded respect for their ancient neutrality and reminded the Athenians of the economic advantages they received from that neutrality. They pointed out that the losses that Athens would have to suffer to overwhelm Melos would not be compensated by the difference between what they would get from the *status quo* and what they would get after a military victory. Moreover, destroying Melos would cause other neutrals to turn away from Athens. But the Melians discounted their own military feebleness. For their part, the Athenians discounted the costs of military victory. Neither side bargained. The Athenians conquered by force, and as the Melians had warned, the little the Athenians gained was more than offset by the resentment they built up among neutrals. But as the Athenians had warned, the fight ended with every Melian man dead and every woman and child enslaved. Thucydides blamed both sides for not sufficiently considering what the balance of power and interest entitled them to.

In September 1938 Adolf Hitler summoned Austria's chancellor, Kurt von Schuschnigg, to Berchtesgaden for an ultimatum. He demanded that Schuschnigg appoint the Nazi Artur von Seyss-Inquart to the Austrian cabinet and practically agree that Germany would absorb Austria; if not, Hitler warned, the *Wehrmacht* "would not stand idly by."[2] Schuschnigg caved. Germany absorbed Austria without firing a shot. Thucydides, and common sense, would have us lay more blame on Schuschnigg than on Hitler.

Consider the balance of power. What would a war to annex Austria have cost Hitler? What could Austria have done militarily to raise that cost? Schuschnigg might have replied to Hitler with certain concessions pleasing to German public opinion and then begun realistic preparations for military self-defense. If Austria had thrown its inferior military power into the balance, what sort of deal could it have extracted from Hitler? Millions of Austrian lives were *not* at stake. Under no circumstances imaginable in 1938 would Hitler have done to Austria what he did to countries he occupied during the war, much less what Athens did to Melos. German public opinion would not have tolerated much harm to Austria. After all, Hitler's propaganda was telling Germans (with some reason) that Austria yearned to be part of the Reich. Almost any kind of resistance would have made Hitler look bad. So the balance of power, rightly understood, should have dictated that Austria's response to Hitler's demands contain a military component. But because Schuschnigg never threw that component into the balance, Austria got a worse deal than it might have.

The key, then, is balancing power and interest. In some cases, bluff aside, the great power can temper its demands, gain a negotiated surrender, and forgo the cost of fighting. In 1940 Nazi Germany presented Denmark with a combination of overwhelming force, determination (in its war with Britain,

Germany *had* to control the Danish straits), and apparently reasonable demands: the Danes would grant the Germans passage to the straits and in turn would receive a gentle protectorate. The Danes gave in without a fight. Later the Germans chose to be ungentle.

In other cases, fighting is unavoidable. In May 1940, as in 1914, the Germans had to go through Belgium to defeat France. But in 1940 they could not lull the Belgians into surrender, because the Belgians remembered all too well German occupation a generation before. So Germany had no alternative but to spend blood and iron attacking the Belgian fortresses.

In 1940, what did Germany want of Switzerland, and what force was it prepared to use? Germany did not need to go through Swiss territory to attack any major enemy. Nor did it fear attack through Switzerland from any major enemy, much less any Swiss attack. The Nazi regime would have liked to incorporate the two-thirds of the Swiss people who speak German dialects, and it urgently wanted to stop the flow of hostile commentary from the German-language Swiss press. But these were not military necessities. Even though Germany absolutely needed to ensure its uninterrupted innocent traffic to Italy through the Alpine railroad tunnels, military operations were unnecessary for that; the treaty of October 13, 1907, between Germany, Switzerland, and Italy guaranteed that traffic, and no one imagined the Swiss would violate it. Of course the Germans would have preferred to send troops and weapons through the tunnels as well, going beyond the treaty. But that would have required a full-scale invasion, of which the tunnels might well have been a casualty. The Germans must also have wanted the fruits of Switzerland's precision manufacturing industry, and an invasion would have enslaved the makers of Swiss watches.

But while slave labor can run assembly lines, it was by no means sure that slaves could produce anything as good as what Germany could buy from free but economically constrained Swiss. Germany also needed access to an accepted neutral currency and banking center, both of which would have been destroyed by an invasion. Besides, if Germany won the war, Switzerland would fall into its hands as a matter of course. Most important, while Switzerland made no urgent claims on Germany's military resources, lots of other places in the world did. Hence, German military planners put a low priority on invading Switzerland.

What about Switzerland's objectives in the Second World War? Absolutely, the primary aim was to avoid German occupation and to retain as much independence as possible. But how could this be secured *militarily*? If Germany had wanted to occupy Switzerland, the Swiss army could not have stopped it. The Swiss military could only have *raised the cost of a German military invasion*. How high that cost had to be to avoid invasion depended largely on the claims on Germany's forces elsewhere. It also depended on the extent to which Germany could achieve some of its goals in Switzerland through political-economic pressure backed by the threat of force. Managing the effective height of the threshold would thus depend only in part on the Swiss army's military capacity.

Some historians have argued that there was no real threat of a German invasion because in fact Germany never decided to invade. For instance, revisionist historian Hans Ulrich Jost argues: "Neither the High Command of the *Wehrmacht* nor the political leadership ever envisaged a conquest of Switzerland. On the contrary, in economic and military circles the operation was generally discouraged."[3] According to this logic, Swiss military planning was a kind of vain self-indulgence. Yet this argument is based on the *post hoc* fallacy; one may not argue that an event could not have happened only because in fact it did not happen. Why *did* responsible German military and economic leaders advise against an invasion of Switzerland? Could their judgment have had anything to do with the comparison between the cost and benefit of such an invasion? When human beings desire anything, they invariably find that it will cost some effort to obtain it. Therefore you cannot assume that when human beings do not reach for something they really do not want it, any more than you can believe the proverbial fox who called "sour" a bunch of grapes that were out of easy reach. Moreover, since Germany had invaded any number of small countries, it was hardly unreasonable for the Swiss to assume that they might be next.

Swiss military planners sought to provide one and only one element of what their country needed to avoid an invasion. Some historians portray a split between those military leaders who were more willing to confront the Germans militarily and those more inclined to propitiate them with political-economic concessions.[4] Yet this distinction is largely false. After the fall of France in June 1940, all recognized that any fight with Germany could only end in defeat. After that date, all Swiss professional controversies about military policy were strictly about how, not whether, to lose and die. Whether Switzerland's defeat came slowly or quickly, whether it was costly or not for the aggressor, would determine the country's honor and therefore its future. Still, the point was to avoid the fight. Despite the serious professional and personal disputes among them, Swiss military leaders agreed, to a man, that their preparations would have to be part of an overall strategy including political and economic disincentives to invasion.

Switzerland's supreme commander, General Henri Guisan, not a professional soldier but a farmer, was a French speaker, a Francophile, chosen for his post because of his visceral anti-Nazism. Writing after the war, he had every incentive to burnish his already glorious reputation for stressing military resistance over concessions. Nevertheless, Guisan began the report on his tenure as follows: "I understood that the role of the Army was to offer to each of the belligerent parties a sufficient obstacle so that adding the force of the military argument to that of political and economic arguments, it would discourage aggressive designs."[5]

Colonel Ulrich Wille, Jr., was very different. A Swiss general's son, a German speaker steeped in Germanic culture, and a professional soldier whose ambition to succeed his father was negated by Guisan, Wille so despised his chief professionally that he actually plotted against him. Yet his views on the role of the army were identical to Guisan's. At the crucial June 22, 1940, meeting of the High Command, Wille did argue for demobilizing more troops so that the Swiss economy could more quickly satisfy German economic demands. But at the same time, as well as at the July 6 meeting, when Germany's victory seemed certain and accommodationist feeling was at its height, he and his Germanophile staff argued that Swiss troops ought to deposit their weapons in a mountain redoubt that would be a harder nut for Germany to crack because it "would not permit the movement of large [German] units any more than of Stukas."[6] Four days earlier Wille's close associate and intellectual guide, the equally Germanophile Colonel Hans

Frick, had written to his chief: "[I]f there is yet something left for us to throw into the balance against exorbitant German demands, it is the army and only the army. . . . In the conditions in which we now find ourselves we have need of radical [military] solutions if we want to survive with honor."[7] In sum, according to nearly the whole spectrum of Swiss military thinking, accommodation and military defiance were inextricable parts of the same strategy.

The following is the story of how the Swiss army helped its country achieve its great objective by manipulating one variable—the military cost of invasion. This is a story of maximizing a few assets and finessing many liabilities—of making lemonade out of lemons. The story begins with Switzerland's military tradition, its preparation for the Second World War, and the brutal reality check of June 1940. After that we will follow the process by which the Swiss arrived at their stark deterrent strategy and look at the value of the military instrument they built. Then, after considering the role of Swiss intelligence and intelligence in Switzerland, we will examine the army's role in combating subversion within its ranks and in society. The Swiss army's political contribution to the country's spirit of resistance to defeatism was arguably more important than anything it did in the purely military field. An army's heart and mind are often its most important weapons.

Military Tradition and Preparation

It is not unusual for mountain country to breed fierce, clannish fighters. Of the ancient Helvetians, Julius Caesar wrote, *"Cum virtute omnibus praestarent"* (They stood above all others in [military] virtue).[8] During the Holy Roman Empire the Swiss cities were known for upholding their rights against greater nobles by keeping military stores to ride out sieges, and for raising tenacious militias. Indeed, the Swiss Confederation dates from a 1291 meeting of representatives of the cantons of Schwyz, Uri, and Unterwalden in response to oppression from the powerful southern Germanic princes of the house of Habsburg. During the Renaissance, when mercenary militias rented themselves to most of Europe's princes, the Swiss acquired a reputation as unusually tough pikemen. In 1512 Machiavelli wrote that Swiss infantry had not once suffered defeat, either from cavalry or from other infantry.[9] The relative valor of these troops may have been due to the fact that, whereas other mercenary bands were made up of scattered riffraff, the Swiss units consisted of people who had grown up together and stood by one another. Swiss mercenaries were also prized as bodyguards. Louis XVI's Swiss guards died to the last man in his defense. To this day the pope is guarded by a Swiss force. In the old sections of Swiss cities, tourists can still see the homes built by the mercenary contractors.

With the beginning of the wars of the Reformation, fewer Swiss fighters ventured abroad. Nevertheless, some Swiss mercenaries continued to fight abroad, as far away as Britain's war against the Zulus in 1879. Since their valleys now contained both Protestant and Catholic cantons that lived in uneasy peace, the Swiss were eager not to add to the power of foreigners who might come and break that peace. This is the beginning of Switzerland's neutrality, which began in fact in the sixteenth century, in name in the seventeenth. Moreover, though the Swiss had become known abroad as military professionals, Swiss territory was characterized by the age-old militia tradition. Every able-bodied man would be expected to fight for his community with whatever weapon he could bring.

But this combination of parochial focus and military nonprofessionalism served the Swiss less and less well as their neighbors consolidated into states, ever bigger and better armed. Throughout the seventeenth and eighteenth centuries, Switzerland's recurring military problem was that the professional armies of France or Austria, trying to get at one another, would traverse or even appropriate a Swiss canton. The militia of the affected canton would be too little, and help from others would be too late. The cantons would sometimes find it easier to get help from the other major power than from other Swiss. At the height of Louis XIV's power at the turn of the eighteenth century, they even dealt with faraway Britain. Because of the looseness of their confederation, the Swiss were prey to subversion as much as to bigger armies. Still, the Swiss Confederation did maintain a kind of armed peace with the whole world from 1521 to 1798.

By the end of the eighteenth century the wars of the French Revolution brought bigger armies and more subversion than the confederation could handle. Gradually, Switzerland lost all but a façade of independence and became a French satellite. The French incorporated the Valtellina into their newly formed satellite, the Cisalpine Republic (the present Italian province of Sondrio). The French also occupied the Geneva area. Bonaparte freely traversed Switzerland to fight in Italy. And the cantons were divided internally by French propaganda about liberty, equality, and fraternity. So, when a French army marched on Bern in February 1798, it did not meet serious resistance. The Swiss were required to supply contingents to the Napoleonic armies. The only Swiss military feat of the age came on October 12, 1812, when a detachment sacrificed itself covering the French crossing of the river Berezina at the start of Napoleon's catastrophic retreat from Russia.

Modern Switzerland

In 1815, when the Swiss Confederation reemerged from the Congress of Vienna with a formal guarantee of neutrality, it sought to create a military instrument to guard its neutrality. Until 1848 the central government could only request that the cantons supply a single army from throughout the country. The federal government's executive consists of a Federal Council, whose members are each in charge of a department—for example, the Military Department, the Political (Foreign Affairs) Department, and so on. The ceremonial post of president of the confederation rotates among the federal councilors. The country's bicameral parliament is much less powerful than ordinary legislative bodies, because the Swiss people make most decisions on important matters by referendum. But when war among neighbors threatens to spill over into Swiss territory, the councilor on military affairs proposes, and the parliament elects, some military officer to the wartime rank of general, a rank somewhat reminiscent of the ancient Roman constitutional office of *dictator*. The general asks the Federal Council to mobilize the army. Mobilization is a momentous step because it takes out of the economy nearly all men of military age. Therefore, during extended military emergencies like World Wars I and II, the general and the Federal Council have to negotiate about how much of the army is to be rotated on and off active duty. The general, however, has the authority to use local contingents as seems best for the whole. In 1874, heeding the lessons of the Austro-Prussian and Franco-German wars, the Swiss created a General Staff and modernized military operations, at least to the point of relieving soldiers of the cost of their rifles. But the militia tradition continues: every man a soldier. Indeed, not until World War II would soldiers be compensated for the loss of their livelihoods. But even then, Swiss cavalrymen had to bring, or pay for, their own horses.

Even casual visitors to Switzerland have been impressed by the extent to which the country is militarized. Any weekend of the year, the railroad stations are full of civilians-turned-soldiers for training. They leave their automatic weapons piled up on the platform. Nobody but foreigners pays attention. Or you can see policemen nodding politely to men walking out of banks with machine guns—reservists must keep their personal weapons at home, and they often take them to work on the way to training. Troops are accustomed to guns from childhood. Switzerland is the only country other than the United States where guns are easily bought. While other European men play cards or golf, Swiss men are likelier to enjoy target practice. The country has few golf courses but many shooting ranges. Ever since 1657 the city of Zurich has had a three-day holiday, called *Knabenschiessen*, to introduce twelve-year-old boys (and now girls) to shoot. People of all ages can be seen bicycling through the streets with guns slung on their backs, heading for shooting sport.

On his twentieth birthday every able-bodied man becomes liable to at least nineteen days' military service every two years for a period of twenty-two years. Higher ranks must serve until age fifty-two, or (for higher officers) sixty-two, and in emergencies until age sixty-five. Swiss men are also required to take part in an "off-duty shooting program." At the end of service, they get to keep their personal weapons. Conversations with men at the top of Swiss society quickly uncover that, in contrast with their counterparts in Europe or America, their knowledge of military affairs is deep and their sympathy is lively. A successful professional in any field is almost surely a field grade officer of infantry, artillery, or combat engineers. Once I was interviewed by the anchorman of the French language television news, who happened also to be a colonel of artillery. Nowhere else in the West (Israel excepted) would that have been the case.

The Swiss armed forces are also unlike others in that, even in modern secular times, they emphasize the Christian duty to fight to the death for their community. Swiss secularists find other sources for patriotism. Nevertheless, anyone familiar with the professional military literature of modern Europe and America cannot help but be shocked by Colonel Pierre Altermath's article in the November 1995 issue of *Revue Militaire Suisse*, entitled "Long Live Our Militia System!" The article cites Martin Luther's well-known blessing of bearing arms to protect others, repress evil, and safeguard the faith. It cites Jesus' "No greater love hath a man than that he give up his life for his friends," as well as St. John's admonition to love in deed as well as in word. The prophets Ezekiel and Habakuk, as well as contemporary spiritual guides, are also cited in support of the main point: We Swiss men are committed to our duty to fight and die for our country. While there is nothing unusual about such an article in Swiss military literature, there is nothing remotely like it in modern Western military literature *or practice*. Imagine, then, the state of mind of Swiss soldiers in earlier times.

The Swiss army that mobilized 250,000 frontline troops for World War I was technically on the same level as the armed forces of its neighbors. Switzerland's army was seriously motivated, socially solid, and technically competent. Its senior officers had attended the war colleges of France and Germany. Its heavy artillery was the German 120 mm from the Franco-Prussian War, while the field artillery consisted of the French mainstay, the 75 mm. The machine guns were good local models. And the Swiss were well dug into trench lines on their northern and western borders.

Yet on the eve of World War I no one imagined that the Swiss army would stand up to any of its neighbors' armies alone. In 1907, when France seemed the likelier aggressor, Swiss Colonel Theophil von Sprecher exchanged memoranda called *Punktationen* with the German army detailing the conditions of collaboration in case of a French invasion. By 1917, however, when it appeared that Germany might want to use Swiss territory to bring to bear against France the divisions newly released from the Russian front, the same von Sprecher initiated talks with the French General Staff. In short, Swiss neutrality depended mainly on the willingness of Switzerland's neighbors to deprive one another of the advantages of going through Swiss territory. The Swiss army would help by forcing any attacker to mount a major offensive and by delaying success long enough for help to arrive. But the Swiss always made it clear that help would not be welcome a moment sooner than called for.

Swiss men of military age spent World War I rotating from civilian life to the trenches. While in uniform, they suffered under the harsh Prussian training regimen of their general, Ulrich Wille. When at home, they suffered hunger and increasing poverty brought on by the loss of traditional international trade, especially a drastic drop in agricultural imports. Only farmers got rich selling foodstuffs at scalpers' prices. Social cohesion suffered. Meanwhile the Swiss read about the far worse sufferings of their French, German, and Italian brethren beyond the borders. By war's end the Swiss people shared— albeit to a lesser extent—the antimilitarism and revulsion to war

that characterized the rest of European civilization. Like elsewhere in Europe, Swiss cities were filled with Socialist demon-
strators and with the cry "Never again!" In 1918, much as in
Germany, Marxist-led demonstrations threatened to overthrow
the government. In 1932 Swiss troops had to break up a Socialist demonstration, shooting and killing eleven people. In short,
in the years after World War I, even the Swiss were less mindful of military security than usual.

That is why the Swiss people narrowly approved entering the
League of Nations in 1920. The Swiss conditioned their mem-
bership on the special assurance that they would not be required
to take part in any war. Thus did they think that they could reconcile engagement with neutrality. Indeed, in Switzerland as
elsewhere the League was sold to voters not as an obligation to
go to war to safeguard other peoples' rights, but as assurance
that "the league" as a whole would somehow safeguard each
member's rights—another set of reasons for mindlessness about
military matters. When the League reacted to Italy's 1935
takeover of Abyssinia by driving Switzerland's Italian neighbors
to the south into worrisome cooperation with its German
neighbors to the north, the Swiss revived the notion of armed
neutrality.

Before the Storm

The illusion that the Great War had ended wars faded more
quickly in Switzerland than elsewhere. As we will see, Adolf
Hitler was much less a mystery to the Swiss, especially to the
German-speaking majority, than to other nations. Nor was the
idea of rearmament as shocking to the Swiss as to other Europeans and to Americans. In addition, while other countries
were cursed with bad leadership during the 1930s, the Swiss

drew some unusually good cards, including Rudolf Minger, who became head of the Federal Military Department in 1930. In the first two years after Hitler came to power, Minger raised the defense budget from about 95 million francs to about 130 million. In 1935 he went beyond the budget process, directly to the public, proposing an issue of defense bonds worth 235 million francs and campaigning for direct purchase by the public. The Swiss people responded by buying 335 million francs' worth of the bonds. By 1939 another 171 million was added. By referendum, the Swiss agreed to lengthen military retraining and to extend the age of military obligation for the lower ranks to sixty. So, on the eve of World War II, a nation of 4.2 million people stood ready to field an army of 440,000 men backed by a corps of 150,000 armed volunteers over sixty or under eighteen years of age, and another 600,000 civilian auxiliaries.

By the outbreak of war, new weapons were beginning to come into service. But, like most other armies that had not guessed the character of modern, mechanized warfare, the Swiss had not bought wisely. The Swiss, like most everyone else, envisaged a replay of World War I.

The combined air corps and anti-aircraft corps had bought fifty excellent German ME 109 air superiority fighters. But because the General Staff was blind to the use of aircraft to support ground operations, Switzerland had bought no bombers and no ground attack aircraft, like the Stuka. As for anti-aircraft artillery, the Swiss had four Vickers and four Schneider 75 mm guns, plus thirty-four modern Oerlikon 20 mm weapons. The mission of the combined air and anti-aircraft forces was to protect Swiss airspace and Swiss airfields, but if the ME 109s had tried to fight for air superiority, they would have been swept from the skies by sheer numbers. More likely, they would have been destroyed before ever leaving their undefended airfields. Forty-two AA guns were obviously insufficient for defending airfields or anything else.

Moreover, the ground forces were not equipped for modern warfare. Each battalion had only one infantry cannon that could be used against tanks, plus just two grenade launchers. Obviously, the idea of armored warfare had not crossed Swiss planners' minds. The war for which they had planned would have consisted of shooting oncoming infantry from border trenches. To that end there were sixteen thousand machine guns, four hundred French 75-mm field guns, entirely horse-drawn, and only fifteen 120-mm guns. In addition, there were various small caliber mountain guns. The only motorization for the infantry came from commandeered civilian vehicles (a maximum of 15,000 taken away from the civilian economy) plus 50,000 horses taken away from agriculture. Pictures from that time show rows of machine guns hitched to a variety of taxicabs and family sedans, smartly lined up. The Swiss cavalry rode horses.

The strength of the army lay in its 440,000 men, organized in six infantry divisions, three cavalry divisions, and a half-dozen brigades, and in the good, deep fortifications and trenches the Swiss had built along the borders. About one-fifth of the army would occupy these positions, while the rest would wait close behind the German and French borders ready to rush to wherever the attacker might be. The earthworks would absorb the enemy's artillery fire, the defenders' machine guns would take their toll, and the main army field divisions' counterattacks, including those by the horse cavalry, would keep the enemy out of the country—until help could arrive.

The first news of the German campaign in Poland showed all this to be a pipe dream. The German armored spearheads had sliced through the kind of army that Switzerland had. The intellectual process by which the Swiss adapted to their new circumstances is of more than historical interest.

On August 30, 1939, the Swiss parliament activated the wartime post of "general" and entrusted it to Henri Guisan. The new general instantly complained that there was no plan for operations. But no strictly operational plan could fit the Swiss army for the circumstances in which events were plunging it. Guisan's first response was to pull the army back from the strictly artificial border fortifications to ones resting on terrain features.

Contrary to the belief of those who do not look at maps, Switzerland has only its *back* to the Alps. The roof of Europe shields Switzerland only from the south and the east—that is, from Italy and substantially from Austria as well. From the west—that is, from France—Switzerland is moderately accessible through the Rhône valley and across the hills of the Jura. But the north and northeast of Switzerland, bordering on Germany, are open, rolling plateaus crossed by gentle rivers and lakes. Three-fourths of the Swiss people are located in these accessible regions, as well as the preponderance of their industry and agriculture. This non-Alpine Swiss terrain is better for defensive tactics than northern France—but it is also pretty good tank country. By contrast, the steep valleys of the Alps are natural fortresses. Of course, only one-fourth of the Swiss people live there. In sum, Switzerland's terrain can be useful for defense, but only to the extent that the defenders can exploit it under any given technological conditions and against a given kind of opponent.

A glance at the map of Switzerland *(fig. 1)* shows that a nearly straight line of rivers and lakes roughly parallels the northern border, from the Rhine at Sargans in the east, following the

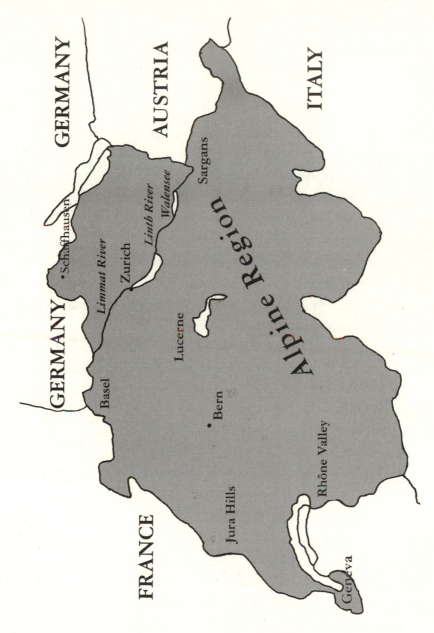

Figure 1

Wallensee, Linth, Zurich Lake, and Limmat almost to the Gempen plateau above the Rhine near Basel in the northwest. Guisan ordered most of the army to pull back behind these waters and dig in, while keeping the border troops in place. But this new plan left some 20 percent of the country open to occupation, including Basel and Schaffhausen, and put the biggest city, Zurich, right on the front line. It also meant that the costly border positions would henceforth be useful only to slow the enemy a bit. Yet events would quickly show even this sacrifice to be grossly insufficient—the Swiss military would be driven much farther down this path of logic.

The general's arrangements for help from France would turn out worse. Conventional wisdom had it that the only strategic choice facing Swiss military commanders was whether to deploy the preponderance of forces in the north (against Germany) or in the west (against France). Like most of his countrymen, Guisan never had any doubt that the threat came from Germany. But the country's formal neutrality, as well as the presence of high-ranking officers who would have been happier if the threat had come from the other direction, obliged Guisan to act formally as if he were dispassionate about his basic strategic choice. Hence he had to plan with the French in secrecy. Guisan was personally acquainted with top French officers such as Gamelin, Georges, and De Lattre, with whom he had toured the Maginot Line. As go-betweens he used Major Samuel Gonard, who had studied at the *Ecole de Guerre* in Paris and who traveled there often as a civilian lawyer, as well as Major Samuel Barbey, a novelist who also had good connections in the French army.

The result was an informal but nevertheless written agreement by which the French army would provide artillery fire support to the northwest end of the Swiss army position on the Gempen plateau, and move its own troops there directly to back up the Swiss. The Swiss actually improved roads leading onto the plateau and built revetments for heavy artillery for the French army's eventual use, effectively linking the Maginot Line to the Swiss fortifications. In addition, elements of the French 7th (later the 45th) Army corps would cross the border near Geneva and move northeast. For the sake of symmetry in case of discovery, Guisan began secret exploratory talks with Germany through Major Hans Berly, who had good contacts in the *Wehrmacht*. But these never resulted in concrete plans.

Joint planning with France turned out to be a source of trouble rather than help because France itself fell quickly to the German onslaught, and the records of the Swiss negotiations fell into German hands—among a carload of government documents abandoned by the French and recovered by the Germans at Charité Sur Loire on June 16, 1940. The Swiss worried that Germany would use their breach as a legal reason for disregarding their neutrality. But they need not have worried. If Germany had wanted to invade, a jury-rigged pretext such as the staged border incident with Poland in August 1939 would have been enough. More worrisome was Switzerland's basic military predicament.

By April 1940 the fall of Norway and Denmark showed that German armies could move just as efficiently across water and against Western armies as they had against Poland. No sooner had Germany's attack on France begun on May 10, 1940, than the mismatch between the German and Swiss armies became glaring. In Belgium, en route to France, the Germans opened the way for their mobile forces with parachute troops and saboteurs. German paratroopers could drop onto Swiss fortresses bereft of air cover or air defense as easily as they had on the Belgian fortress of Eben Emael, mistakenly assumed impregnable. Coordinated ground attacks would then overwhelm them. Could the Germans punch through the new Swiss army position on the Sargans-based line? Without antitank weapons, Swiss infantry positions couldn't prevent breaches. And if Swiss troops behaved like other armies, they would panic once the formidable German columns came near. In fact, as France was falling, tens of thousands of Swiss civilians piled mattresses atop their cars and headed for the mountains, pro-Nazi groups were strutting, and no prominent politician could be found to rally the country. In sum, no army can fight without means or hope.

Stiffening Resistance

Thus, even as the Swiss still hoped for help from France and Italy, they studied how to meet the mobility and psychological shock of modern warfare. Since there was no chance of quickly raising the Swiss army to German standards, much less of increasing its numbers, the Swiss could only fall back on bloody tactical resistance to the last man coupled with radical strategic withdrawal.

The psychological effects of German successes had multiplied the effects of German tactics. The proximate objective of all ground combat is to breach the enemy's line and, by ravaging the enemy's rear areas, to cut the opposition's routes home. By these means, an attacker can count on disorganization and discouragement to work wholesale destruction on a defender. The style of mobile warfare introduced by Germany in 1939 had proved effective in this regard. Yet if somehow every defender reacts to a breakthrough by fighting harder at his post—resistance to the last man—the attacker's advantage is minimized. Later in the war Japanese troops forced American soldiers to dig them out and kill them one by one—at great cost in blood, treasure, morale, and time. But it's easier to preach resistance to the last man than to practice it.

Without knowing the Swiss military tradition, one could easily discount Guisan's order to his troops as German forces were breaking through French lines at Sedan. The order attributed "the stunning daily progress of certain troops" (it was politically incorrect to name any potential opponent) to the failure of individuals to do their duty. Hence Guisan ordered Swiss troops to disregard whatever might be going on around them: "Each man, even if isolated, must defend himself where he is. . . . [E]ven if encircled, [units] must fight until the last bullet, and then attack with their blades. . . . So long as any man has a bullet or a blade, he has no right to surrender."[10] Every officer and NCO, regardless of circumstance, was responsible for gathering whatever troops happened to be around and leading them against the enemy. Order after order reminded the troops that the country's authorities were irrevocably committed to military defense, and that any radio transmissions the troops might hear to the effect that Switzerland had given up or that they should do anything but fight to the death were to be treated as the work of the enemy. This drumbeat would automatically brand as traitors any government official or senior officer who might want to throw in the towel.

Guisan's orders stated, "The attacker succeeds not so much because he deploys superior firepower, but above all through the destruction of the defender's will to fight to the end." You are here, Guisan said, to sacrifice your life. To the troops' reasonable question of how they could fight with enemy airplanes all over them, Guisan answered that bombing and strafing from the air could kill you no more dead than artillery. But what about the tanks—they can slice right through our positions! "None of you must quit his post, even if armored tanks are attacking or have already arrived on the flanks or in the rear. . . . You must be confident that our rear echelons will deal with them. . . . So long as you maintain your positions on both sides of the breach, and you do not permit the arrival of reinforcements, these eruptions amount to nothing." And the same went for being outflanked by enemy parachutists.[11] While it was nonsense to say that being penetrated and outflanked was militarily meaningless, it made perfect sense as part of a strategy to hold together the army and to harm the enemy.

It is by no means certain that these orders would have been followed had Germany invaded. But the orders did hold the army together. During the middle of May the Germans massed troops near the Swiss border. This turned out to be a feint, to distract the French from Germany's main axis of assault through Belgium. Nevertheless, the Swiss massed their troops to get in the way. There is little doubt they would have fought. Late in the campaign, as German armies approached the Geneva area, the Swiss massed troops there, while interning the fleeing remnants of the French army on whom they had counted for help.

In the war's crucial period—June 1940 to Spring 1944—Switzerland's military strategy rested on the willingness of its border troops to die and of the bulk of the entrenched army to take casualties without hope of relief. Even to plan such operations takes a certain bloody-mindedness. Yet we should not conclude that willingness to die is necessary only in desperate circumstances. Rather, it is a necessary condition for any meaningful military action.

The only place where Swiss and Germans shot at each other during the war was the airspace over the French border. When 180 German planes violated Swiss airspace, the Swiss shot down nine and lost only two ME 109s in the process. Angered by this, the *Luftwaffe's* commander, Hermann Goering, ordered a commando team to blow up Swiss airplanes. On June 16 Swiss authorities arrested the team. Alas, the Reich soon intimidated the Swiss government into releasing the team, the captured German pilots, and the remains of the airplanes that had come down on Swiss soil. The Swiss government even added an ambiguous apology. In short, the Swiss military had bravery and skill—but little else.

Reassessment and Redoubt

If the fall of France had been unimaginable, Italy's entry into the war on Germany's side was counterintuitive. True, the general European assumption that Mussolini would follow Italy's natural geopolitical interest in limiting the power of Germany had taken a beating in 1938, when *Il Duce* failed to bolster Austria's feeble resistance to the *Anschluss*. But in 1940 even Winston Churchill thought that Mussolini would know his interests well enough not to join Hitler.[12] In Switzerland, conventional wisdom had been that Mussolini would do whatever was necessary to avoid having northern Italy surrounded by a stronger power. Therefore Italy, like France, could be counted on to help maintain a Swiss buffer. Swiss leaders in 1940 were heirs of a foreign policy that had adjusted Swiss interests with Mussolini's Italy very well. So in June 1940, when Mussolini added the weight of forty million Italians to that of eighty million Germans, the military predicament of four million Swiss could not have been worse or more unexpected. The country could be attacked from all sides and expect help from none. The greater part of the Ticino canton, including the city of Lugano, became indefensible, just like Geneva, Lausanne, Fribourg,

Bern, Basel, and Zurich. Indeed the question became, could the Swiss army defend anything for any useful purpose?

The events of June 1940 forced the Swiss to confront the question that no military establishment anywhere wants to confront: What would we do if we found ourselves alone, relying strictly on our own resources, against a first-class enemy? Most countries build their military forces to fight the wars they would prefer to fight—not the ones they dread. And yet the foremost military lesson is that armies should prepare first and foremost for fighting alone against the worst of enemies. Switzerland's plans to march a screen of heavy infantry around threatened borders loudly proclaiming neutral self-sufficiency while silently arranging for help from large, modern foreign forces was no sillier than, say, American Cold War plans to fight a ground war in Europe against the Soviet Union. Equally silly was ancient Athens's supposition that it could commit the fleet that made it the world's greatest sea power to supporting a major land war in faraway Sicily. Similarly foolish, American post–Cold War plans essentially assumed the friendship or forbearance of most of the world, and that no nation would use nuclear armed missiles seriously. Again, most nations' military plans assume that allies will play a very large role, and that the enemy will not do his worst. What happened to Switzerland in June 1940 taught lessons that have had to be learned time and again throughout history: The availability of allies is inversely proportional to the need for them, and yes, the enemy can be very efficient.

Once military planners accept that they must rely strictly on their own resources, they no longer ask, "What kind of war would we like to fight?" but rather: "What kind of war do our resources allow us to fight? What are our real possibilities? Are we strongest on land or on the sea? Where does our strength lie?" In the case of the Swiss, there really was only one answer: Much as we would like to defend our country against all comers, we must recognize that if we play all our cards right we can hold out for a time—and that only in the Alps.

Consider the topography of Switzerland *(fig. 2)*. The northern part of the country consists of the broad end of the Rhine valley. The west is the broad end of the Rhône valley. The northwest is the broad Aare valley feeding into the Rhine. The southern tip consists of the Ticino valley. In the lower middle is a mountainous mass resting mostly on the Italian border. In the middle of this mass is the St. Gotthard Massif, from which roughly the Rhône heads west, the Rhine east, and the Ticino south. This is the roof of Europe, where Italian, French, and German ethnicities meet. This is the home of the 1 percent of Swiss who speak the ancient Romansch language and live in picture postcard settings. At their beginning, these valleys are high, narrow, and steep. The natural use of this topography for defense consists in blocking the three valleys at the points where they broaden, while also blocking the passes that lead to them laterally from the north and south.

Controlling the main entrance from the south involves blocking the St. Gotthard pass—easy enough in the summer, and no job at all during the eight snowy months. The Swiss had built a fortress guarding the pass. The other passes into Switzerland from the south, guarded by mountains like the Matterhorn and Monte Rosa, are militarily impracticable. At the northeast entrance of the Rhine valley is the fortress of Sargans, while the St. Maurice fortress guards the Rhône entrance to the southwest. The northern lateral gateways into the region are short, steep, Alpine valleys through places like the Bernese Oberland, difficult enough to travel without military opposition. The only

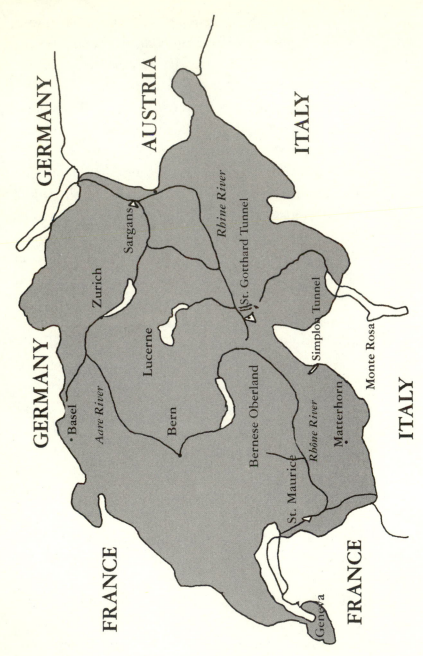

Figure 2

partial exception is the valley leading up and south from Lake
Lucerne.

Here then was an area into which any army could fruitfully
concentrate its defensive resources, however limited. The great
shortcoming of this natural bastion is that it contains little to
defend: its great metropolises have names like Chur, Brig, St.
Moritz, and Andermatt, better known for skiing than for economic productiveness. While it did not take genius to notice
this natural redoubt, it took a peculiar combination of single-
mindedness and desperation to use it as the Swiss ended up
doing.

Here we must return to the central point of the German
army's assessment of what it would take to defeat the Swiss in
1940: only about as much as it had taken to beat the Belgian
army—*unless* a substantial portion of the Swiss army should
manage to fall back into the Alps. Indeed, the first draft of the
German contingency plan for the invasion of Switzerland, dated
June 25, 1940, says that "a well-ordered retreat into mountainous regions" would "retard the military decision." Twice more
that summer, on August 6 and 12, German staffs produced versions of the plan. The differences between them lay in the number of divisions assigned, their precise objectives, and the line
of demarcation between German and Italian forces. The final
version, which bears the signature of General Franz Halder,
chief of the *Oberkommando Des Heeres*, cut the number of divisions to be employed from twenty-one to eleven, while raising
the number of armored divisions to four. But the primary military objective remained the same: to get behind the Swiss army
fast enough to "prevent the retreat of the Swiss divisions massed
on the northern frontier in the high mountains."[13] By January
1944, after the Swiss army had in fact fortified its Alpine region,

the German military attaché in Bern wrote that conquering it would be a difficult task. But by then Germany's big worries elsewhere had become even bigger. Indeed, in 1944–1945 the same German officers who made these judgments about the Swiss mountain redoubt believed that their own best chances against prevailing foes was for themselves to retire into the Alps.

One of the oldest truths of military science is that an outnumbered army that withdraws in good order into narrow places *ipso facto* reduces its exposure to just the entrances, where it forces its superior pursuer to fight on even terms numerically and at a tactical disadvantage. Thus the Spartans delayed the Persians at Thermopylae, and Demosthenes' Athenians stood off the Spartans on Pylos's rocky beach.[14] At the least, defeating a Swiss army ensconced in its mountains would cost time, resources, and embarrassment. Such an army would surely interrupt traffic through the St. Gotthard and Simplon tunnels, and would likely blow them up. In the worst case it could launch counterattacks for years, making it difficult to profit from occupying the rest of the country. It would also provide a focus for resistance in the heart of Europe while Germany was still facing deadly foes. *This worst case would be most likely if the Alps were to be occupied not by whatever remnants of the Swiss army had managed to escape the German armored pincers, but rather by an undefeated Swiss army that had established itself in the redoubt, amassed supplies, and built fortifications.* This became obvious to Swiss and Germans alike. Yet for the Swiss army to avail itself of advantages so natural, so rational, required some unnatural, even irrational decisions.

After June 1940 there was no question in any Swiss military mind that if the Germans attacked, the Swiss army sooner or later would be broken and its remnants forced to take refuge in the Alps. No one questioned the need to prepare supplies and fortifications to receive this remnant—the greater the preparations, the more credible Switzerland's pretense to independence. The objections were about all the unpalatable conclusions to which this logic led: Most of the population would be abandoned to the Nazis' tender mercies, much of the country's productive capacity would have to be blown up, and, perhaps worst of all, the very preparation of such a drastic course would provoke Germany to be harsher toward Switzerland than otherwise.

The logic of Swiss military decision-making after France's defeat flowed from this question: Should the country use armed force to maintain its independence? On June 26, 1940, the day after the French Armistice went into effect, Marcel Pilet Golaz, federal councilor of the Political Department (foreign minister), who was acting as president on rotation, made a radio address to the nation that, though it did not say anything terribly explicit, sounded to many like a declaration that Switzerland would henceforth be a German satellite. The following chapter will describe the political struggle for the country's soul, and Pilet Golaz's part in it. But here the focus is on what the speech meant to the army. Some of the soldiers agreed that the war was over and that they were now truly useless. Others, including nearly all officers, yearned to maintain independence and sought a way to bolster the army's credibility through some kind of national redoubt. The High Command (General Staff, along with the four commanders of corps) met on June 22 and again on July 6 to draw up plans that would make some sense for the encircled nation. Even though there were violent disagreements on what, precisely, the new plan would be, everyone recognized that any plan that was reasonable militarily would involve saving the army at the expense of the country—indeed, destroying the country in order to save it—and that it would not be easy to implement.

General Guisan did not at first support the most radical plans. But the day after Pilet's unfortunate speech, he laid the political basis for any such plan by formally asking the Federal Council if his mission was still to defend the country's independence. An answer of "no" would have meant his resignation and a firestorm of protest across the nation. When the council gave its *pro forma* affirmation, Guisan delivered a set of military prescriptions. These amounted to taking the country's military policy back to very painful basics. By July 12 Guisan had issued the following order:

> Switzerland will be able to avoid a German attack only if the German High Command calculates that a war against us would be long and costly, that it would uselessly ignite a new set of struggles in the heart of Europe, and would upset the execution of their [other] plans. Henceforth the principle of our national defense is to demonstrate to our neighbors that war [against us] would be a long and costly enterprise. If we are drawn into the fight, the point will be to sell our skin as expensively as possible.[15]

In other words, having given up the notion that they could defend Switzerland, the military leaders now focused strictly on deterring attack. To demonstrate their commitment to fight without hope of victory, they had to prepare to do a lot of things—abandon and destroy infrastructure—that they, never mind the politicians, had no heart to do.[16] In the deliberations about deterrence, an aide to General Guisan brought up Pericles' speech to the Athenians when Sparta was first about to invade Athenian territory at the outset of the Peloponnesian

War. Pericles had said that if he could, he would have Athenians themselves destroy the houses and orchards that lay outside the walls, to show the Spartans that Athens cared less for those things than for its ultimate objectives.[17] Acceptance of that logic led to ever more radical versions of the redoubt plan.

While military officers quickly agreed that they ought to sell their own skins, they were not at all agreed about how much of society's skin they ought to be putting on the block. To build and stock this "National Redoubt" would cost a great deal. But the population living outside of it would not be allowed in. Worse yet, the army would turn the routes leading from the borders to the redoubt into traps for the enemy. This would ensure fighting throughout the country. Old men and boys in the civilian population would fight, and draw horrid reprisals. The army, moreover, would mine roads and bridges, even factories, just like the Alpine tunnels. Blowing up everything outside the redoubt that might be of value to the Nazis would leave the civilian population destitute.

Guisan, backed by Francophone upholders of the Swiss militia tradition, objected that he had come into the army to protect the country, not to wreck it. Corps Commander Fritz Prisi talked of the army's duty to die trying to do the impossible job of protecting the population, and thereby inspire future generations. Prisi and his supporters agreed to deploy many troops in the redoubt and to fortify it, but argued that the army should put its main effort into a gallant stand, if not at the borders then on the Linth–Zurich fallback position. Those who escaped destruction could then fall back into the redoubt.

On the other side were the German-speaking professional officers, led by Ulrich Wille and former Chief of the General Staff Jakob Labhart, who argued that any lives lost outside the redoubt would simply be wasted. Death would be more quick than gallant! Why fight, or threaten to fight, in any but the most advantageous circumstances for themselves? Why make the redoubt a refuge for stragglers rather than a potent military asset? Wille in particular wanted to achieve the maximum deterrent effect by putting the country's entire stock of arms and unit headquarters into the redoubt while at the same time demobilizing the army to peacetime levels, to give Germany maximum incentive to have peaceful economic relations.

The middle ground, advocated by Guisan's chief of staff, the professional artilleryman Jakob Huber, stressed practical consider-ations. Of course the redoubt had to be more than a refuge for stragglers; it should be made potent. But since the Swiss army could not possibly stay mobilized for long periods of time, and therefore would need time to remobilize in case of attack, the country could not simply leave its borders undefended. Some troops had to sacrifice themselves to buy time for men to leave civilian life and flow into the redoubt. Moreover, since the Linth-Zurich system of fortifications already existed, why not make use of it to slow down and inflict harm on the enemy? By the same token, why not set up mini-fortresses along the main roads, to make every bend in the road, every bridge and overpass a source of casualties for the invader? Let the invader arrive at the gates of the redoubt already bloodied. Besides, it would take months to dig and pour and stock the redoubt. In the mean-time, the Swiss had better make good use of current positions.

The professionals, however, objected that now was the time of greatest danger, when the Germans most needed to be con-fronted by evidence of Swiss determination.

In a nutshell, on July 10 Guisan chose a version of the middle position. Two-thirds of the army were released from active duty. Order #12 of July 12 wholly reorganized the army deployment.

The new scheme used the term "redoubt" only indirectly; instead the order referred to "echeloning in depth"—the border brigades would slow the invader and die at their posts. Four divisions (reduced to three in the fall) plus three light brigades would then engage the attacker on or near the lines established between September 1939 and June 1940. Finally, they would fall back into an "Alpine position or national redoubt." There they would join five divisions (six in the fall). The troops in the redoubt would have "provisions for maximum endurance" and would hold to the end "without thought of retreat."[18] (Guisan might have added, without *possibility* of retreat, either.) The redeployment would be completed by August, but construction and supply would take much longer.

The plan did not rouse significant civilian opposition even though it stated explicitly that the civilian population would not be allowed to flow into the redoubt. The Federal Council accepted the project largely because the head of the Military Department, Rudolf Minger, proposed it as his own, and other members of the council were unwilling to oppose a senior colleague. But there is evidence that the government might have accepted an even more radical version, since Pilet Golaz had agreed with Wille that even more troops should be dedicated to the redoubt. True, throughout the war, opinion surveys showed that many people did not understand that the redoubt meant they would be abandoned to occupation. But in the critical summer of 1940 the hazy idea of the redoubt gave hope to a desperate nation. At any rate, the Swiss population rallied to the recruitment of old men and boys to fight as "local guards," each with a rifle, an armband and a mere forty-eight rounds of ammunition. More significantly, the country did not balk when, on May 24, 1941, General Guisan issued Order #13, pulling all but the border troops into the redoubt. On the other side of the ledger, although the army did a lot of mining of civilian infrastructure, the scorched-earth policy did not become official until 1943.

It is important to note here that, as the Germanophile professionals had argued, Switzerland most needed its national redoubt in the summer of 1940, just when it was least possible to make it effective. By late 1943, when the Swiss army had fully built the redoubt, the country's military situation had improved to the point that it became prudent to move troops closer to the borders again.

The Military Redoubt

The back-to-basics logic of defending the Alpine redoubt led to a wholesale rebuilding of the army.

To begin with, it required a radical change in the army's plans for employing aircraft. At the outset of war, Swiss aircraft were intended to keep foreign ones out of Swiss airspace, much as Swiss ground forces were to prevent foreign soldiers from stepping onto Swiss soil. But the fifty modern Swiss fighter planes were even less capable of securing Swiss airspace than the army was of securing the ground. True, during May–June 1940 Swiss pilots had established a favorable attrition ratio of better than three-to-one against German planes that had violated Swiss airspace. But even at that ratio, a German invasion would have used up the inventory of Swiss planes quickly and without benefit to Switzerland. Any serious attempt to use the Swiss fighters to prevent Allied bombers from crossing Swiss airspace would have ground down the Swiss air force just as quickly and would have aided the Germans. So, what good were airplanes?

In fact, aircraft became a key part of the Alpine redoubt. By the end of the war, Switzerland had acquired from Germany or manufactured 328 modern Messerschmitt 109s and Morane 3801-02 fighters, as well as 202 C36 bombers. They were based entirely within the fortified region. Many were hangared in tunnels. Their job was twofold: protect the fortified region against enemy bombers and paratroops, and support Swiss ground forces' efforts to hold the gates to the redoubt.

Modern weapons have not invalidated the concept of fortress; they simply require that any given area be protected against modern weapons by modern weapons. By the end of the war, Switzerland's stock of modern 20 mm anti-aircraft tubes had passed two thousand, and long-range 75 mm anti-aircraft tubes numbered more than five hundred. Anti-aircraft batteries were concentrated in the Alpine region in general, and on the three fortresses and airfields in particular. Belgian fortresses had fallen to the Germans so easily because German aircraft had been able to fly over them with impunity. But if the Germans had tried to drop paratroopers onto the Swiss fortresses, or even to bomb them, the surrounding mountains would have forced the attacking aircraft to fly along narrow corridors. After 1940 Swiss fighters from within the redoubt might have been waiting for them around every bend, with anti-aircraft guns hitting them high and low from mountain and valley alike. Operating from behind friendly mountains, the Swiss aircraft would have darted in and out of the envelope of their own anti-aircraft guns to control the skies over the gates to the redoubt and to bomb the enemy on the ground as well.

Switzerland's terrain dictates that military forces going toward one of the entrances to the Alpine redoubt cannot easily shift laterally to go up another valley. By the same token, defensive forces within the redoubt could not easily shift their weight from one sector to another. The bomber force therefore proved to be the most economical means by which the Swiss high command could reinforce any particularly hard-pressed sector. The bombers' advantage consisted in part of their own relative safety. To bomb Germans approaching the redoubt from the ground, the Swiss bombers had to expose themselves to a hostile environment for only a few minutes before ducking back behind their mountains. A force of more than a hundred bombers, seconds from secure areas, could have had a fearsome effect. More recently Egypt, in its 1973 Sinai campaign, stymied Israel's tank-plane assault by quickly covering its advanced positions with a network of SA-6 anti-aircraft missiles, from behind which inferior Egyptian pilots were able to fight the Israelis with some advantage.

The Swiss defense of the redoubt began at the border. Each sector, corresponding to a valley leading to an entrance to the redoubt, was entrusted to an army corps. The corps headquarters and most of the troops were located in the redoubt. But the corps would manage the border troops' delaying action, as well as the work of the demolition troops, the light brigades, and the mini-fortresses along the invasion routes. By the end of the war, the weapons in the hands of these light brigades had become serious. Foremost, these troops were now riding primarily motor vehicles. Swiss forces also possessed some three thousand antitank tubes of various kinds, plus some five hundred self-propelled heavy guns. Even the horse cavalry was equipped with antitank rocket launchers.[19] The job of the ground forces outside the redoubt was to wage a hit-and-run war of attrition against the invader. In this war the Swiss forces outside the redoubt would seek to mingle with the enemy, fighting at short distances to deprive him of the opportunity to use his superior artillery.

This sort of warfare implied a very different sort of infantry from the one at the beginning of the war. No longer would masses of men be delivering small amounts of fire along a static front. Now, small groups would have to dart into (and with luck out of) loose enemy formations, delivering a blast of fire against trucks, tanks, and even aircraft. Infantrymen would thus have to be trained in a variety of crew-served weapons, as well as in the tactics of small-unit warfare. They would have to be motivated in ways very different from those of European parade ground armies. In short, Swiss warfare outside the redoubt could only be guerrilla warfare. General Guisan's final report relates that he tried to turn every Swiss infantryman into a commando.[20]

For most of the war, however, the primary job of forces outside the redoubt, other than sacrificing their lives, was to mine and destroy infrastructure, and indeed to protect the destructive devices against German commandos who might try to disable them. Most important of the minings were those of the Gotthard and Simplon tunnels. Once destroyed, these twenty- and twelve-kilometer (respectively) tunnels and their viaducts would take a decade and enormous resources to rebuild. Protecting the multiple dynamite charges in the tunnels was especially difficult since every day between one hundred and two hundred German and Italian trains lawfully traversed them.

To make sure that the trains did not stop near the mined points, Swiss troops had to be inside the tunnels as they passed. (There are amusing accounts of the tunnel troops being sprayed with the effusions of latrines.) Just as important, Swiss troops had to inspect the trains before they entered the tunnels to make sure no men were in them who could overpower the Swiss guards. At the same time the Swiss made sure that the trains carried no weapons or troops. Indeed, the only Axis troops who ever transited the tunnels did so lying down, having been certified as sick or wounded.

In sum, by the end of the war the new Swiss army would have been able to put up better resistance in the open field. But its leadership had concluded that because no amount of *absolute* improvements could ever erase the Swiss army's *relative* inferiority, the country would forever have to base its military strategy on the assumption that it would have to stand alone, and on taking advantage of its terrain. Guisan wrote: "Our militia army . . . will never be up to successfully confronting the first impetus of a foreign professional army in the open field, unless the terrain on which we rely has been reinforced."[21]

Intelligence

Sometimes, superior intelligence operations can make up for other kinds of military inferiority. Swiss intelligence enjoys a mythic reputation, as does the role of intelligence gathered in Switzerland. But while it is as true as it is natural that much information and intrigue flowed through Switzerland because that nation offered sojourn in the middle of Europe to refugees, spies, and diplomats from all sides—and especially because Switzerland was a convenient drain for leaks from Germany—it is by no means true that the Swiss were terribly well informed or that the information and intrigue that flowed through their country played more than a marginal role in the outcome of World War II.

Prior to 1938 the Swiss intelligence service—over and above the units in each division that sent out scouting parties and interrogated prisoners—consisted of two officers. In 1938 the number grew to three and then five. By the outbreak of war there were ten people, including clerks. At the height of the war Swiss intelligence employed 120 people. By the end of the war the number was down to sixty-six.[22] The original service provided the army with a very basic cryptologic system. To this were quickly added officers with good connections to foreign sources of facts and rumors. Then came people who kept up order-of-battle information on foreign armies on maps of the world. More specialized officers kept up with reports on the technical features of foreign weapons. Other than a section of officers who kept in contact with the corps of foreign military attachés accredited to Bern—and indeed with the network of Swiss attachés and diplomats abroad—the collection side of Swiss intelligence consisted of five offices, in Basel, Zurich, Schaffhausen, Lucerne, and Lugano, from which officers met their contacts, who were overwhelmingly walk-ins. This sort of passive collection was more effective in Switzerland than elsewhere because foreign intelligence services and their "facts" ceaselessly flowed through the country. Swiss intelligence did not consist of Swiss spies who infiltrated enemy organizations. Indeed, the parts of Swiss intelligence that are most often written about are the semi-official outfits established by individuals that got their information by taking what their anti-Hitler friends in Germany would give them. It is worthwhile to examine the worth of all this for Switzerland and for the Allies, and the lessons that can be drawn.

The first lesson is that if an intelligence service fails to give its government what it needs most, that government would likely be better off without intelligence—regardless of what else intelligence might do. The flood of information about the war's various theaters flowing through the country made Swiss officials perhaps the war's best-informed spectators. *But, insofar as Switzerland was a participant, it really needed the answer to one question: When and where would Germany attack, if at all?* In this regard, Swiss intelligence twice did its army almost the worst that any intelligence service can—it passed on reports of possible impending attack that turned out to be wrong. In mid–May 1940 it reported German saber-rattling south of the Black Forest. It should have noted that the Germans were making uncharacteristically open moves southward while actually preparing to move northwest. Worse, in March 1943 Swiss intelligence passed on as real an unsubstantiated rumor that Germany was preparing to invade Switzerland. In reality, the German High Command had no such agenda. The ploy led Swiss intelligence chief Roger Masson to foolishly ask his friend SS General Walter Schellenberg about the agenda, thereby confirming that someone in the German High Command had been passing information to the Swiss.

Worst of all, in 1940 Masson gave secret briefings to members of the Federal Council warning that Germany might invade if the Swiss government did not curb the country's anti-Nazi press. Thus he unwittingly lent himself to Germany's subversion of his country.

Nor was Masson the worst mishandler of intelligence in Switzerland. In 1941 Masson sent the government a report from a variety of foreign sources showing that the Germans were reading communications between the Political Department (Foreign Office) in Bern and Swiss diplomatic missions abroad. Instead of being grateful, the head of the Political Department complained that military intelligence was complicating his delicate relationship with Germany!

The second lesson is that when a government fails to establish a serious intelligence service of its own prior to war, it must then rely on whatever arrangements and networks private citizens may have. Note that America's Office of Strategic Services (OSS) began as an extension of Colonel William Donovan's private contacts. Since the Swiss had no real service prior to the war, their wartime intelligence was dominated by the private contacts of Hans Hausamann and Max Weibel. Because they were reserve officers, General Guisan simply assigned them to run their own networks in loose coordination with Roger Masson's official intelligence shop. Hausamann's operation, known as the *Büro Ha*, received information from long-standing contacts in Germany, some of whom were high in the government and opposed Hitler. In addition, the *Büro Ha* funneled to Guisan the well-informed reports of Rudolf Roessler, a refugee German journalist who had become a major anti-Nazi political commentator under the name Hermes. Roessler shared with the Swiss some of the apparently timely and valuable information on German plans that he communicated to the Soviet Union, where he was code-named *Lucy*. In sum, both for the sake of Switzerland's own intelligence and for that of the Allies, Swiss authorities had to be quite permissive of foreign intelligence within their borders—with the exception of espionage against Switzerland.

As a businessman who spent much time in Germany, Hausamann had been so shocked by the rise of Hitler that he had turned to journalism to warn his country. He wrote and published a book on the need for defense against Germany and produced movies on the same theme, at one time buying up every projector in the country. A man of the political right, he spent so much effort preaching rearmament to Swiss Socialists that he acquired friends and sympathy on the left. His rightist friends in Germany transmitted to him—by nonelectronic means—information from a variety of high-level contacts, including one of their number who worked in Hitler's communications office.

But note well: Hausamann's dynamism did not cause information to flow. That cause was high-level, anti-Hitler sentiment in Germany. The *ReichsicherheitHauptamt* (headquarters of Reich security) was aware of this network of conservative high-ranking anti-Hitler officers and dubbed it the "Black Orchestra." Hausamann called his network into the right-wing anti-Hitler underground "the Viking Line."

Then in 1942, one of Hausamann's leftist friends put him in contact with Roessler, whose information apparently also came from former military colleagues who had risen in the *Wehrmacht*. So, Hausamann was the recipient of two excellent military networks. Although the political coloration of Roessler's sources was unclear, Roessler himself also transmitted his intelligence through Sandor Rado, a Hungarian Communist living in Switzerland as a cartographer and running an intelligence radio relay service from Lausanne to Moscow. At the beginning of the war, Rado's organization, known as the Dora ring, was the main part of Moscow's intelligence in Western Europe that had not been shut down by the Stalin-Hitler Pact. After mid-1942 Dora was functioning as the last surviving piece of the famed German Communist spy organization, Leopold Trepper's "Red Orchestra." Thus Switzerland in general and Hausamann in particular were at the crossroads of the two main lines of espionage coming out of Germany.

In addition, Max Weibel was receiving information from the anti-Hitler element of *his* former classmates in Germany's war college, while the *Abwehr's* chief, Admiral Wilhelm Canaris, was passing information to the Swiss as well as to the Allies through the German vice consul in Zurich, Hans Gisevius, as well as through a young Polish refugee, Halina Zymanska.

Then, beginning after the great German defeats of 1943, a panoply of German officials, ranging from the plotters who would eventually try to kill Hitler on July 20, 1944, to emissaries from Himmler himself, were contacting the Allies in Switzerland.

The German government was aware of an intelligence hemorrhage through Switzerland. Direction-finding radio receivers had established that nightly encrypted traffic was emanating from the Geneva area. Cryptological analysis showed that the messages were from Dora to Moscow, and that the information was important. Germany pushed the Swiss government hard to shut down Dora. But this did not happen until the ring was betrayed from within, leaving the cantonal police no choice.

The relevant question must be: To what extent did Swiss intelligence, and its provision of a permissive environment for intelligence favorable to the Allies, make up for the weaknesses of the Swiss army? Some of the information that went from Roessler through to Moscow about the *Wehrmacht*'s plans at Stalingrad and Kursk was of the highest importance, as was a lot of data on German war production. One *Büro Ha* runner would sometimes bring to the British Embassy material from Roessler about German U-boats. Yet none of this made the difference between victory and defeat at Stalingrad, Kursk, the Atlantic, or anywhere else.

Nothing that Switzerland did or allowed in the field of intelligence made up for the fact that it was a tiny country. Hence the answer must be that intelligence by and through Switzerland played more or less the role that one might have expected given the country's geographic position and the circumstances. The pressure of events—rather than anything that Swiss intelligence or America's spymaster in Switzerland, Allen Dulles, did—was what increased the flow of intelligence. After all, the greatest flow of intelligence out of Germany began after the Battle of Stalingrad, when not only anti-Hitler Germans but Nazis as well became anxious about how to avoid the worst for their country and themselves. One of the timeless lessons regarding the role of intelligence is that information tends to flow to the side that is believed to be winning.

Counterespionage, however, helped the Swiss military cause considerably. We have no way of knowing what percentage of German agents the Swiss managed to catch or what percentage of Switzerland's military secrets Germany was able to get. Given the extent of the German network, Germany must have done very well. Nor is it clear how or to what extent Germany's knowledge of Swiss military preparations would have helped it in case of invasion. But beyond doubt, German intelligence feared Swiss counterespionage. A German officer summed it up this way: "After a certain point the Swiss counterespionage organization was considered as by far the most dangerous. It is in Switzerland that the proportion of agents put out of action was highest. Our painstakingly built networks were constantly disorganized by timely interventions of Swiss counterespionage."[23] Over the course of the war the Swiss arrested approximately 1,400 persons for espionage, of whom 328 were sentenced to long prison terms, while 33 were condemned to death for spying for Germany; 15 of these men were executed, including three Swiss officers.

The respect for Switzerland that these executions engendered among Germans was less important than the favorable impression they made on the Swiss population in general and the army in particular. The country felt put upon, robbed, humiliated, frightened by the Germans. Killing spies working for Germany was a small yet concrete way of affirming the country's integrity and will to independence. The first death sentence was against a sergeant who sold the Germans, among other things, sketches of some minor fortifications along one of the roads leading to the redoubt. Historian Hans Ulrich Jost, in his book *Nouvelle Histoire de la Suisse et des Suisses*, argues that the Swiss establishment agreed to the executions "as if to expiate the feeling of guilt that permeated the highest ruling circles."[24] Certainly some of the businessmen who were making money dealing with the Germans, or some government officials who cowered before Nazis, were more reprehensible and more consequential than petty spies. But the willingness to kill spies signified to these very businessmen and officials that collaboration had better be kept within limits. Above all, if the country was willing to kill its own citizens for any kind of collaboration whatever, it was likely to resist an invasion.

Indeed, the foremost military question was whether the country as a whole *would* resist. Hence the army's most significant battle of the war was precisely against those whose commitment to resist was shaky, as well as against outright subversion.

Subversion and Politics

The greatest threat to a besieged army is subversion of morale and policy by uncertain high-ranking officers and civilian authorities.[26] This is the kind of treason that none dare call by its name because it so often prospers. Next to it, the subversive activities of foreign agents is small stuff. Not surprisingly, before the defeat of France foreign agents had little luck because Switzerland's leadership was resolute and its national unity was greater.[26] But in 1940 the danger came from the weakness of domestic leadership. Switzerland's battle against subversion then became a *military* campaign for the country's soul.[27]

The Nazis set about subverting Switzerland as they had sub-
verted Germany, Austria, Czechoslovakia, and the rest. They
organized a core of semi-professional party toughs who would
intimidate ordinary people through threatening marches, street
violence, and fiery rallies. At the highest political levels, Nazi
leaders worked to convince the Establishment that it was futile
to resist. In Switzerland the first part of the plan failed miserably.
The second nearly succeeded as a result of Germany's preponderance in 1940–1942.

Switzerland's Nazi Party, which had been active since 1934,
was under orders from Berlin to agitate for an *Anschluss* to unite
the German Swiss with the Reich.

Several things went wrong. First, the Swiss authorities made
it impossible for the Nazis to commit the acts of intimidation
that had served them so well elsewhere. Second, and most
important, very few German Swiss joined the organization; in
fact, Nazism was less distasteful to the French-speaking cantons
than to the German-speaking ones. Finally, on February 4,
1936, Wilhelm Gustloff, the leader of Switzerland's Nazis, was
assassinated, and the Swiss government refused to allow any
Swiss citizen to succeed him.[28] A year later, the Swiss government officially made the German Embassy responsible for the
party's actions. Under this scrutiny the party vanished into
insignificance. Its members were tracked by the Swiss police,
and by 1940 the party had dissolved.

During the mid-1930s the entire Swiss establishment, including the trade unions, recognized that Nazism discredited the
very idea of a multiethnic state, of democracy and economic
liberalism, as well as of centuries-old civil liberties—everything
that Switzerland stood for. Nevertheless, there were narrow
limits to what a liberal government could do to counter massive
propaganda from a totalitarian neighbor. Plans for a Swiss

propaganda ministry came to nothing. But the government established a private foundation, *Pro Helvetia*, to drum up Swiss patriotism. It sponsored movies, speakers, and the successful Zurich National Exposition of 1939. Almost as an afterthought, the organization established a military branch, Army and Hearth. This was to mean nothing until the outbreak of war, and nearly everything thereafter. During the late 1930s, as country after country was falling under the Nazi spell, Switzerland enjoyed an outburst of patriotism. In March 1939 Swiss Economics Minister Hermann Obrecht pledged that, in contrast to other European appeasers, no one from the Swiss government would "go to Berchtesgaden" on pilgrimage to Hitler. His statement was widely applauded.[29]

So, until the fall of France, worries about fifth columns were vastly overblown. On May 14, 1940, when a German invasion seemed imminent, the Federal Council ordered the arrest of every politically active German, plus all prominent Swiss Nazis. It's a tribute to Swiss liberty that the order was countermanded when the invasion did not come.[30] In short, in patriotic Switzerland traditional Nazi subversion failed as nowhere else.

Germany's military successes in 1940, however, undermined Swiss confidence. Germany's defeat of France, and its apparent defeat of Britain, seemed to validate every bit of the Nazi critique of European liberalism and to augur a collectivist future controlled by Germany (together with the Soviet Union). Nazi Germany's New European Order offered rebirth through peace, order, work, social security. "What's the point," asked some sophisticated Swiss, "of being the only ones to resist the New Europe with utter futility and disregard for our safety—for the sake of what has failed?" Patriotic defiance, and the Alpine redoubt, seemed a thin answer.

To forbid Switzerland from saying out loud that Germany was its enemy, the Reich combined the threatening reality of its overwhelming force with the blandishment of a parent toward its mischievous child. The German Embassy and the German press were accusing Switzerland of violating its neutrality by allowing expressions of dismay at Germany's victories, and by insufficiently appreciating the virtues of the Nazi political system. Moreover the Swiss press was introducing into German discourse all sorts of mockery of Nazism. For example, it parodied the Nazi claim of crusade, *kreuzal,* into *hakenkreuzal*—twisted cross-ade. By so doing, the Germans maintained, Switzerland was contributing to the loss of German blood (*Blutschuld*). Germany threatened to reevaluate its respect of Swiss neutrality if Switzerland did not fix the problem. The Swiss Establishment's preference for complex, fuzzy ways of looking at a challenge whose face was too fearsome, and its inability publicly to identify the enemy who threatened the country, undermined cohesion in the armed forces and society.

By July 1940 the Swiss troops believed that, regardless of what their general was saying, neither the government nor even their own senior officers would give the order to fight. When they went home, they absorbed the civilian environment's tendency to accommodation. Above all, it was not clear that accommodation with Germany or even with Nazism was any longer wrong. Perhaps those who were opposing collaboration were mere extremists who were endangering the country. Maybe *they* were the real enemy. In a phenomenon all too familiar to Americans who lived through the Cold War, antitotalitarianism became suspect. Consequently, to hold its own soldiers together, the army had to face basic political questions—and set the tone of discourse in the country at large.

On July 25, 1940, General Guisan gathered the army's 650 field grade officers to the spot where the Swiss Confederation had been founded in 1291—the Rütli meadow above Lake Lucerne. There, on sacred ground, speaking solemnly and switching occasionally to heavily accented German, he reiterated the army's duty to defend the country, explained the redoubt plan, and ordered the officers to convey to the troops their own determination and confidence. Although he did not mention the words "Germany" or "Nazi," Guisan condemned faint hearts who would not stand against aggression. The Reich expressed outrage. After the Rütli speech, General Guisan toured the country, spreading the same message. One observer described the general's speeches as subtly "recalling to divine law those who had forgotten the prayers of their youth."[31] For General Guisan Swiss patriotism was next to godliness, and the army was its embodiment.[32]

The army, however, was anything but united. Nor is it fair to characterize the Federal Council as unpatriotic. Yes, it took a softer line than Guisan. But none of its members had Nazi sympathies. Still, public opinion quickly contrasted the Rütli speech, and Guisan's endless tours of the country plus the programs of Army and Hearth, with President Pilet Golaz's uninspiring speech of June 26. The general was on his way to becoming the national hero, credited with everything that went well, while Pilet Golaz and the Federal Council were doomed to be cast as the goats.

Still, the popular perception has an element of truth. Although only a handful of marginalized Swiss were as ready to celebrate their country's defeat as many mainstream Americans ended up being willing to celebrate America's failure to stop Communism in Vietnam, nevertheless army leadership is the reason why many Swiss refused to go along with the Nazi enterprise.

Three of the army's most prominent officers—Hans Hausamann, Oscar Frey, and Max Weibel, friends of the general to a man—had been so shocked by Swiss President Pilet Golaz's June 26 radio address that they formed a secret cell pledged to resist Nazism to the death, regardless of any orders to the contrary. General Guisan discovered the amateurish plot, shook the ringleaders' hands, and sentenced them to punishments that amounted to brief vacations. He did not hesitate to use these officers as the intellectual core of Army and Hearth's programs.

Those programs succeeded in giving audiences what they could not get anywhere else—namely, large amounts of factual information. Army and Hearth provided troop commanders with *Wehrbriefe*, sets of talking points on the evolution of the war and of Swiss defense preparations, explanations of Germany's role in the Swiss economy, discussions of refugee policy, the rationing system—in short, the sort of things that would have come through a free press. In addition, the organization sent professional speakers around to the troops and trained promising troops to be speakers. These speakers were provided with talking points on basic subjects, usually laid out in Thomistic format: propositions (generally those of the accommodationists) followed by objections to the propositions and then discussion. For example, Speech Plan #22, titled "The Jewish Question," set out the basic theses of anti-Semitism and then refuted each one with facts, statistical analyses, and ethical argument.[33] Soldiers were encouraged to tell the folks back home what they had learned.

In the days following France's disaster, many officers became convinced that a direct effort was needed to rescue civilian public opinion. At the end of July the bulletin of Army and Hearth said, "At this time, the officer must become the educator of our people." On three occasions during the summer Guisan asked the Federal Council to lead public opinion to support the army's mission. By the fall the army had taken matters into its own hands. On October 21 Guisan established a civilian section of Army and Hearth, which in the end conducted 328 courses and delivered some 4,000 lectures. The Federal Council tried to starve it for funds, but no matter. The section got its materials, ably written (and *gratis*), from a group called *Aktion Nationaler Widerstand* (National Resistance Movement), which included the general's friends in the army as well as backbench members of parliament. It, in turn, got its authority from the general.

The Federal Council was upset. The Germans objected, especially to Swiss Colonel Oscar Frey's anti-Nazi speeches, given in uniform, to civilian audiences on the border. The Federal Council forced Frey to desist, even as it allowed Nazi Gauleiter (party official) Fritz Sauckel to address the German community in Basel. But recall, this was 1941; Germany seemed sure to win, and it was easy to view people like Colonel Frey as loose cannons who would bring nothing but harm on their country. Yet in October 1942, after a speech by Gauleiter Bohle, chief of all Nazis abroad, to Germans in Switzerland at the Zurich *Hallenstadion*, the Swiss government banned all large gatherings by foreigners. By then, the balance of power was shifting and the Reich's triumph no longer looked so sure.

The Swiss Federal Council also had to deal with objections to the army's role from within the army itself. Colonel Gustav Däniker was prestigious, very well connected, and an admirer of the *Wehrmacht* who thought his general was incompetent and irresponsible. Returned from Berlin in March 1941, Däniker officially requested in May that the council take action against the press for having defamed Germany, as well as against General Guisan for having jeopardized Swiss–German relations. The council took no action. But the very fact that the council had entertained his request showed that a substantial number of high-ranking army officers thought Army and Hearth was doing harm. (Däniker cited as the chief example of the press's irresponsibility reports that the Reich was preparing to attack the Soviet Union. When the invasion occurred three months later, Däniker was discredited and the general was able to relieve him of his command.)

At any rate, to the council the general was no hero. In December 1940 the general's best friend on the council, Rudolf Minger, was replaced by Karl Kobelt, who disagreed with Guisan's approach. In addition, the retirement and death of the council's other senior member, Hermann Obrecht, left the national executive bereft of anti-Nazi hard-liners, leaving the general even more isolated politically. But the public supported Guisan. When the Federal Council banned all pro-Axis organizations on November 19, 1940, it was under mounting public pressure orchestrated by Guisan. In response to violent German protests, on November 26 the council also banned all Communist organizations. The general could not have been happier. In 1942 and 1943 pro-Nazi fronts tried to reorganize under different names. The council was even more harsh, putting their leaders in jail.

In the end, the value of all of Switzerland's military measures, from the retooling of its infantry to the redeployment of its aviation, to its fight against subversion, was determined by events in places like Stalingrad, Kursk, Midway, and El Alamein. Had these battles gone the other way, General Guisan's future might not have been so bright.

CHAPTER 3

Politics

"Democracy is the worst political system—except for all the others."

—Winston Churchill

F OR DEMOCRACIES ABOVE ALL, war is the ultimate election.[1] The prospect of being killed bearing arms for a particular polity, or just for standing by it, forces people to decide
just how much they like it, what price they are willing to pay
to continue living under it. In World War II Swiss democracy
confronted Nazi Germany, a power that denied with seemingly
irresistible, deadly force everything that Switzerland stood for.
Hence the Swiss had to decide in a host of practical ways just
how much they valued independence and their way of life.

Even more than the United States of America, Switzerland
is renowned for democracy. At the national level no less than
in small villages, the Swiss decide public business by referendum. Nowhere else do constitutional law and custom put so
short a leash on officials. And yet, as World War II loomed and
raged, Swiss officials often acted with little regard for democracy
or public opinion. So, as the war went on, the Swiss government largely lost the confidence of the people. The outsized
popularity of General Guisan was the reverse side of the widespread loss of faith in government.

The System

Switzerland doesn't fit the mold of the traditional nation-state. The two-thirds of the Swiss people who live in the northern end of the country, the Rhine and Aare valleys, speak Germanic dialects. Their literary heroes and villains, their philosophical categories, come from the broad traditions of Vienna, Dresden, Cologne, Kiel, Berlin, and Bonn. The roughly one-fourth who live in the upper Rhône valley and west of the Sarine River speak French and look at life through a lens focused on Paris. The one in twelve Swiss who live in the Ticino valley and the Grisons canton speak Italian and partake of the culture of Dante and Manzoni. The rural Grisons on the Italian and Austrian borders is also home to the Romansch minority, who are closest to the Helvetians of the Roman Empire. Just as important, each city and valley has its own dialect and its own traditions of independence. Although all schools teach at least two Swiss languages, most Swiss live physically, intellectually, and emotionally in their own linguistic communities, knowing little of the others' textbooks, entertainers, newspapers, radio, and TV personalities. In reality, Switzerland is composed of four civilizations, twenty-six semi-sovereign cantons—six of which count as half cantons but are in almost all respects equal to the others—and about three thousand self-governing localities.

Forging any sort of unity out of such diversity would be impossible except for the very widespread sense that the rest of Europe has been going to the dogs for centuries, and that only the wise, moderate, old-fashioned Helvetian inhabitants of Europe's headwaters have a grip on an ancient, decent way of life. The Swiss take great pride in their differences from the rest of Europe.

First among these is, precisely, diversity. But note, the Swiss tolerate their country's differences so well because each can retreat into a small community in which there are few if any variances. People trust one another on the basis of their ability to speak dialects or with accents peculiar to their tiny localities.

The second Swiss distinction from Europe is freedom, secured by an armed people. The third is economic liberalism. Even though no stranger to Europe's collectivist trends, Switzerland is always several degrees more liberal than its neighbors.

Thus, though a *Valaisan* takes his intellectual bearings from Paris, he is typically repelled by the thought of being submerged in a large state exclusively with other French speakers and ruled by economically *dirigiste* bureaucrats. For him, living with a majority of *SchwyzerDeutsch* is emphatically not like living under Germans. The Germanic population is even more committed to Swiss independence—especially from Germany. After all, the desire to get away from powerful German princes was the original *raison d'être* of the Swiss Confederation. But also, whereas French Swiss are confident of cultural equality with other Frenchmen, if not with Parisians, the Germanic Swiss know that they will always be seen as highland bumpkins by the *Hochdeutsch*. Only in Switzerland can the Germanic Swiss be first-class citizens. As for the Italian speakers, they may be the most fervent patriots of all, knowing full well how much worse life for them would be if they were dominated by the corrupt culture of the lower peninsula. The Romansch are uniquely Swiss. Ultimately, every Swiss prizes the opportunity to stay aloof from the quarrels of large nations. All in all, this engenders a powerful nationalism sometimes rendered insufferable by pretensions of moral superiority.

Because of its diversity, freedom, liberalism, and direct democracy, Switzerland abhors central power—especially executive power. It is not unusual for the people (to whom scholars and journalists commonly refer as "the sovereign") to reject proposals made by vast parliamentary majorities, or to approve motions disapproved by the political establishment. A 1991 referendum rejected Switzerland's moving to join the European Union, ardently advocated by the whole political establishment. As for the executive, each department of government functions under its own chief, responsible to the parliament. At the outbreak of World War II there were (and there remain today) seven departments: Political (foreign affairs), Military, Interior, Justice and Police, Postal and Railroads, Public Economy, and Finances and Customs. Together, the chiefs of the departments constitute a Federal Council that collectively exercises executive power. The presidency rotates among the council's members. In Switzerland the Federal Council acts by mutual deference and consensus, if not unanimity. Consensus on the need for consensus produces strong (some say stifling) pressures for moderation.

As in other democracies, political parties bridge the separation of powers. In the Swiss case (as in the case of the present European Parliament of Strasbourg) they also bridge the different nationalities. Through the first two decades of the twentieth century, German, French, and Italian Swiss elected more "radicals"—traditional European liberals—than any other party. The other major parties were the Farmers, Workers, and Citizens—an agrarian party—and the Catholic Conservatives, a kind of Christian Democratic Party. By the 1930s the Socialist Party was gathering more votes than any of them—some 28 percent—but still the other three parties excluded it from the Federal Council. The three parties shared the seats on the Federal

Council, appointed major bureaucrats, and developed ever closer relations with the country's economic powers. For good or ill, they were the country's Establishment, and had begun to build a kind of oligarchy.

The Swiss parliament formally elects the Federal Council every four years. In practice, the leaders of the major parties, who are often members of the council, are the leading elements in the "political chemistry" that proposes candidates to the parliament to fill any vacancy among council members. When the parties propose and parliament elects a new federal councilor, they try to maintain a roughly proportional representation of the major cantons, of the three nationalities, as well as of the major parties. So important is maintaining these balances that the members of the council often shift portfolios amongst themselves to accommodate the proper new member in a proper role. In 1940, for instance, when longtime Foreign Minister Giuseppe Motta died, Enrico Celio was nominated to replenish the council's ranks—lest the Italian region lose its sole representative on the council. But since the wartime Foreign Ministry required experience that could have come only through service on the council, the position went to the then Postal and Railroads minister, Marcel Pilet Golaz. All the regions and government parties agreed.

The Swiss government gained power in the years leading up to the war because of the dangers of the world crisis and the apparent success of Swiss statesmanship. In 1939 the Federal Council was led by Motta, an unassuming man who earned the respect of the League of Nations, built what seemed a solid relationship with Mussolini, and kept Hitler at bay. Then there was Hermann Obrecht, who left a profitable banking career to craft his country's economic survival in the coming war. And there was Rudolf Minger, the Bernese farmer whose rebuilding of the army reminded people of Cincinnatus. These humble patriots' habits and manners inspired trust unmixed with fear. Why not put the country's fate in their hands?

On August 30, 1939, the same joint session of parliament that elected General Guisan also voted "full powers" to the Federal Council for the duration of the war. In so doing, the parliament appointed a committee fully representative of itself (including Socialists) to oversee the council's exercise of "full powers." But the people's representatives soon learned that the committee members so enjoyed being in on the council's secrets and powers that they would not even tell their parliamentary colleagues—now reduced to the role of uninformed kibitzers—what was going on. With good reason, members of parliament and citizens alike quickly became distrustful.

Specifically, while the Swiss people had trusted the veteran Giuseppe Motta to weave through the quarrels of Europe, they did not have the same trust in the new foreign minister (and president for 1940), Marcel Pilet Golaz. In sum, a year into the war the Swiss people found that the death or resignation of Motta, Obrecht, and Minger had transformed the Federal Council to which they had given "full powers" for the duration of the war into a playground for the vain (Pilet Golaz) and the weak (Justice and Police Minister Eduard von Steiger). One of the perennial lessons of politics is that whereas extraordinary leaders may be safely entrusted with unusual responsibilities, their ordinary successors may not. It is easier, moreover, for a people to give up its local and democratic liberties than to take them back.

The great lesson of the Swiss experience, then, is that the voters' ability to choose between strongly argued alternatives is even more important in emergencies than in ordinary times.

Divisions, Issues, and Consensus

The political system's strong inclination to consensus stopped where the Socialist Party was concerned. In 1918 the Socialists, led by their Leninist wing, led their growing constituency into violent strikes. As Hitler's rise to power was threatening the Swiss, the Socialist Party was demanding the disestablishment of the Swiss army. To the cozy cohabitation of three linguistic communities the Socialists preferred proletarian internationalism. To armed independence they preferred pacifism. To economic laissez-faire they preferred economic redistribution. In short, to the Establishment they represented the negation of all things Swiss.

In the mid-1930s, however, the party underwent major changes. In 1935, largely out of fear of the Nazis, the party accepted the principle that the workers should participate in national defense. In 1937 it led a collective bargaining agreement between labor, capital, and the government that was hailed as "Peace in the Workplace."

Nevertheless, mild and decent as Socialist leader Max Oprecht might have been, and despite all he had done to purge the party of extremists, at the outbreak of the war the other parties still feared inviting the Socialists into the Federal Council. After all, the Socialist Party still contained a Communist wing, led by Leon Nicole. Since Hitler was allied with Stalin, these Swiss Communists were agitating against the Swiss army and making common cause with the pro-Nazi fronts. After the Reich's invasion of Russia, however, the Socialists became the fiercest advocates of resistance to Nazi Germany and expelled their Communist members, whose activities the Federal Council then banned. By then, of course, resistance itself had become very much *the* issue. Hence by excluding the Socialists the traditional parties weakened the country's resolve. Also, since the Socialists were the country's largest party, their exclusion from what was essentially a war cabinet detracted from Swiss democracy-by-consensus. Then again, much of what the Federal Council did during the war had that effect.

In 1943 the Federal Council finally allowed the Socialists to join the government, after the party made big gains in that year's election. The belated entry of the country's largest party into the government meant a return to Switzerland's tradition of democracy, and more. Socialists in the Federal Council were able to correct the Establishment's disastrous policies on freedom of the press and loosen its restrictions on refugees. They also, however, worsened its economic policy. Still, important public choices are better made democratically than by councils of experts, if for no other reason than that elections can remove leaders of bad policy.

Consensus and Democracy

Switzerland's wartime political troubles arose in part from the 1930s consensus on three propositions, largely shared by other Europeans as well as Americans. The first premise was that unemployment poses a mortal and perpetual threat to the good life because there will always be a surplus of workers and a shortage of jobs. Hence the state must take any and all measures to promote and safeguard jobs, including subsidies, currency manipulations, and trade restrictions and preferences. The objective of international economics, then, must be neomercantilism—"beggar thy neighbor." The second proposition held that the people's scarce job opportunities are threatened most directly by immigrant labor. So the state must do what is necessary to drive out foreigners who are stealing jobs and to keep others from coming in. The third proposition was "no more war." The government must do whatever necessary to keep the country out of others' quarrels. For a small country in the heart of Europe in the 1930s, this meant accepting restrictions on freedom and democracy so as not to displease Nazi Germany. The three propositions shared one underlying premise: The State must use all its powers, even arbitrarily, to achieve these goals.

In 1935 the perceived need to steer the economy through the Depression first led the country to accept arbitrary exercise of "emergency" power by elites and bureaucrats. Their liberal democratic virginity gone, the Swiss would then grant their Federal Council even greater powers to deal with the challenges of Nazism and war.

Consider the Federal Council's 1935 request for two years of "full powers" for economic purposes:

Far be it from us to put democracy into question.... In the period of economic distress that our country is now traversing, the government nevertheless has the obligation to neglect nothing to overcome the gravest difficulties.... The existence of our economy is at stake, that is to say the independence of the country. The end sought is of such importance that the parliament and the Swiss people should not hesitate to renounce temporarily the exercise of certain rights, whose exercise is possible only in normal times.... The only way of saving our democracy is to provisionally restrain some democratic and juridical principles, always under the observation of the Federal Assembly and public opinion.... There are circumstances in which it is not possible to respect the letter of the laws and the Constitution. . . .[2]

True. In the 1930s the only economists who disagreed with the proposition that the Depression was caused by an excess rather than a deficiency of government intervention were of the Austrian School—right-wing outcasts. Few if any in the Swiss Establishment, and certainly not the Socialists outside of it, remembered without scorn the pre-1914 conventional wisdom that free international trade benefits everyone. Few argued against the web of restrictions and subsidies that made up the modern economic catechism. Fewer could remember that labor makes wealth, or imagine that in a few years Switzerland (and other nations) would prosper by recruiting foreign labor. Certainly not the Socialist opposition.

So, given such near unanimity, what harm did the Swiss do to themselves by giving up democracy in economic and other matters? Quite a lot. The virtue of democracy is not that any given decision by the people produces good policy. Indeed, Tocqueville reminds us that democracies are prone to lemming-like unanimity in gross errors. Rather, democracy is good because it allows fickle peoples to disown disastrous policies quickly. Responsible as they might be for bad judgments, the people simply blame and sack those who had lately been their instruments. But elites who are personally responsible for bad policy are stuck with themselves, and compound disaster trying to prove that they had been right all along.

Room for remedying bad policy is least when a democratic people puts its "full powers" into the hands of a group that represents all (or most) parties and supposedly takes account of the full spectrum of opinion. (In America such things are called "bipartisan" or "blue ribbon" commissions.) Competition among the Establishment parties—not naturally a hardy plant—withers as the parties' fortunes are merged. The Establishment insulates itself from criticism of its own errors and turns away from disturbing thoughts. As the people lack legitimate vehicles for their dissatisfaction with Establishment idiots, they tend to give their support to strange politicians.

It turned out for the best, then, that the Swiss Federal Council excluded the Socialists for most of the war. The fact that the Socialists had argued against the Federal Council's policies ever since the autumn of 1940 gave the Swiss people a responsible vehicle for their protest.

Let us now look closely at three sets of policies elaborated by a consensus of Swiss experts and hotly contested among the Swiss people.

Überfremdung vs. the Jews

The notion of *Überfremdung*, of being overwhelmed by foreigners, was a legacy of World War I. Prior to that, the nations of Western Europe, and the United States, had been relatively tolerant of immigrants. Then, Woodrow Wilson's attempt to transform the Austro-Hungarian and Ottoman empires into nation-states set off rounds of ethnic cleansing and flights of refugees that threatened to overwhelm welcoming states (and that continue into our time). By 1924, when the Johnson Act sharply restricted immigration into the United States, all major countries of Europe had already done so. Only Switzerland's borders remained relatively open.

Prior to 1914 European governments did not require each others' citizens to show passports at border crossings in time of peace. Ordinary people flowed across borders at will. After 1919 almost every government retained the wartime practice of requiring passports, and even visas. Economic liberalism and free trade had been replaced by the notions of economic autarchy and neomercantilist competition. The Turkish slaughter of Armenians, the Polish pogroms against Jews, the Bolshevik barbarities—all drove into Western Europe thousands of people who looked, acted, and smelled different. As the nations sorted themselves out and the Depression took hold, more refugees were on the way.

Switzerland's diversity and tradition of welcoming refugees made it a magnet in Europe. In the two years after Louis XIV's 1685 revocation of the Edict of Nantes, 150,000 French Protestants flowed through Switzerland, while just 20,000 stayed in Switzerland. After the failed revolutions of 1848 came the persecuted Italians, Poles, and Hungarians. After the failed Russian uprisings of 1905 Vladimir Ulyanov (Lenin) and his Bolsheviks found haven in Zurich.

But Switzerland, one-tenth the size of France or Italy, one-twentieth the size of Germany, could not absorb large numbers of refugees before alarm bells went off. Note, however, that the bells went off while the foreign population was actually *declining*. In 1914, 14 percent of Switzerland's inhabitants were foreigners. By 1920 the percentage of foreigners was down to 10.4, and by 1941, when *Überfremdung* was a big issue, it was half that—about a third of the foreign population that had raised no eyebrows a quarter century before, and a fourth of the foreign presence in the year 2000.

Still, as late as 1939 (by this time with a dose of hypocrisy) Swiss authorities put up a sign in the Zurich National Exposition that read: "Our proud tradition is that Switzerland is a haven for the dispossessed. This is not only our thanks to the world for centuries of peace, but also and especially our acknowledgment of the great enrichment that has been brought to us by homeless fugitives since time immemorial." But the truth was that Switzerland's post–World War I bureaucracy had narrowed the country's open door.

This increased sensitivity to foreigners was not anti-Semitism, because as the numbers of all foreigners dropped, the Swiss allowed the number of Jews to rise. By 1941 Jews constituted the largest group of refugee foreigners. Though few in the Establishment *liked* Jews, anti-Semitism was very much out of fashion. Nor was the issue a shortage of public money, or even of food to care for refugees. Most (at least of the Jewish) refugees were cared for at the expense of private charitable organizations eager to do even more, and although food was rationed during the war, there was no real hunger. Clearly, the active ingredient was a certain set of ideas embodied in the bureaucracy and the Establishment political parties.

Like so many other bad things, it all began during World War I. In 1917 an ordinance of the Federal Council established the Foreigners' Police as a branch of the Federal Department of Justice and Police to coordinate the cantons' surveillance of foreigners in wartime. Alas, government agencies tend to survive the end of the circumstances that called them forth. In 1920 thirty-year-old Heinrich Rothmund brought his dogged bureaucratic skills to the branch and quickly became known for interpreting every regulation in a way that would chase the maximum number of foreigners out and keep to a minimum those coming in. In 1931, as an alternative to quotas on immigration, the parliament approved the Federal Council's broadly worded proposal to give the Foreigners' Police discretion over the residence of foreigners on a case-by-case basis. Of course the council and the governing parties made eloquent statements in support of Switzerland's tradition of asylum for political refugees. Nonetheless, because the law gave the Federal Council, to which Rothmund reported, arbitrary power to determine the meaning of "refugee," it took the whole matter out of electoral and parliamentary politics—much as U.S. law grants broad discretion to the Immigration and Naturalization Service (INS).

Keep in mind, however, that the bureaucrats and ministers justified almost everything they did in this field in terms of defending Swiss labor. Rothmund himself published a magazine article in 1921 listing the kinds of foreigners who would be most useful to the country—those who brought rare skills or capital and who were easily assimilable. The least desirable were the least assimilable and those who would add to surplus skills. He concluded that Jews from the East were least desirable.[3] Nevertheless, because of the Nazis, the number of Jews arriving in Switzerland rose. That is because, however much Rothmund and his friends may have wanted to keep them out, Jews could come in and go out of Switzerland like anybody else.

Economism also shaped Rothmund's reaction to Nazi persecutions. Whereas Hitler attacked his political enemies physically as soon as he came to power, his first act against the Jews, on April 1, 1933, was economic—requesting German citizens to boycott Jewish businesses. Only three days later, Rothmund concluded in a memo to his department head that any Jews seeking permanent residence in Switzerland were not to be treated as political refugees. If they scrambled to flee Germany, Rothmund argued, it was because the Nazis were making life economically and socially difficult for them—not because the Nazis were putting their lives in direct jeopardy.[4] Later he acknowledged that because the Jews were victims of state policy, their plight was somehow political. Nevertheless, their lack of political activity, in short their innocence, disqualified them as political refugees. Rothmund interpreted the category "political refugee" to include only those whose life was endangered as a result of specific political acts on their part—and interpreted it so narrowly that between 1933 and 1942 only about ten persons per month qualified. Other countries were also using the distinction between "economic refugees" and supposedly real ones to keep out foreigners while salving their consciences. Meanwhile, of course, one of history's greatest tragedies was unfolding quite outside of any country's bureaucratic categories.

It would be nice if the experiences of World War II had shamed countries out of this way of looking at refugees. But, alas, in 1994 the United States began returning Cuban refugees to Fidel Castro's Communist regime, claiming they were only "economic refugees." Thus did the United States end the last vestige of its former policy of being a refuge from Communist tyranny. In the European Union of the year 2000, politicians from Britain to Spain vied with one another to limit the number of foreigners seeking a better life or escape from dictators.

We should also remember that in the 1930s it seemed impossible that a civilized state like Germany would kill people because of their ancestry. Indeed, the overwhelming majority of German Jews were slow to take the Nazis at their word. In 1933 about sixty thousand left. By 1935 the flow had shrunk to half that number, and between ten thousand and fifteen thousand Jews actually *returned* to Germany. Only in 1938 did Jews begin to flee in desperation, spurred by the March 11 *Anschluss* of

Austria and by the *Kristallnacht* of November, Hitler's first act of generalized physical violence against Jews. Even then, many remained, believing that the regime's latest outrage against them would be the last. When Hitler came to power, approximately a half million Jews were in Germany; by 1939 about half had left. During the rest of the war only about another fifty thousand managed to get out to destinations as far away as China.

How did the Swiss respond to this flow of refugees? Until 1938 the Swiss never considered refusing *entry* to anyone from a neighboring country; the restrictions were on the right to take up permanent residence. Despite the Foreigners' Police, there are no comprehensive statistics on the number of Jews who passed into Switzerland. We know that in 1933 some 10,000 German Jews were registered. In 1936 the canton of Bern officially had 638, but the cantons did not necessarily have accurate figures or report accurately. That year, one Swiss Jewish agency reported having helped 2,400 Jews and counseled another 800. The best estimates for the mid- to late-1930s were of 12,000 fugitive Jews in the country at any one time.[5] It appears that between one in six and one in ten Jews fleeing Germany went through Switzerland. It was, of course, geographically more convenient for most to go through France, Belgium, and other countries.

With the *Anschluss* the stream of Jewish refugees became a flood. Beginning in March 1938 Swiss policy—"official preference" would be a more accurate term, since no screening at the borders was yet possible—was to admit only those Jews who had reasonable prospects of moving through to another destination. Swiss authorities were briefly delighted when President Franklin Roosevelt called for a conference of thirty-two countries to find homes for fleeing Jews. The conference opened in Evian, France, on July 9, 1938. Switzerland, represented by Rothmund, offered to be the staging area for the exodus. But no country, including the United States, would take significant numbers.

This posed a special problem for Switzerland because, almost alone in the world, it did not require visas for border crossings. Its reputation as a haven began to draw an ever-increasing proportion of Jewish refugees to its borders. In July and August 1938 alone, 4,600 Jews entered the country without means or prospects of moving on. In 1938 it was all too easy to project the July and August numbers into *Überfremdung*. Swiss officials therefore sought some means of restricting entry to those who could show that they could move elsewhere, or to well-off retirees who could remain in Switzerland without taking anyone's job.

Swiss officials began to restrict entry by imposing bureaucratic restrictions. This began with instructions to border police not to honor any Austrian passports (invalid under international law since the *Anschluss* had extinguished Austria) unless stamped with a visa from a Swiss consulate. This in turn allowed the consulates to screen out Jewish refugees. But many consulates, notably the one in Rome, issued visas to Austrian Jews anyway.

Jewish refugees with German passports posed a bigger problem. Switzerland could not simply impose a visa requirement on all Germans. Nor did any Swiss official want to put his name to a policy of exclusion of Jews *per se*. Nor did any Swiss official want to abet the Reich's discrimination against Jews, much less do anything that might imply or entail discrimination against Jewish citizens of Switzerland. Nevertheless, while most Germans crossing into Switzerland were likely to go home again, Jewish Germans crossing into Switzerland were likely to stay. Not even Rothmund objected to large numbers of Jews coming in. But there was support for limiting the number of any and all permanent refugees. And in 1938 permanent refugees were Jews. So Swiss officials threatened the Reich with the inconvenience of a universal visa unless it did something, anything, to channel the flood of Jewish refugees away from Switzerland. Since Reich policy (until the beginning of the war) was to push Jews out, German officials were not eager to solve Switzerland's problems. On September 29, 1938, however, the Reich responded by stamping the passports of Jews with the letter "J." This allowed Swiss officials to subject these and no other German passport holders to the equivalent of a visa requirement. This would seem perhaps the most concrete example of a policy aimed exclusively at Jews. But of course the Jews were the only border crossers likely to stay indefinitely. This visa requirement in turn nearly shut off the legal flow, except of course from those who found consulates and border guards that would ignore the new rules.

The bigger challenge to the bureaucratic policy came from the combination of the refugees' desperation and the humanity of the Swiss people. As soon as legal access to the border was shut off, the illegal border crossings began. Many of those caught were forced to sneak back into Germany as best they could. Others were handed directly to the German authorities as Swiss border residents watched in horror. Others were allowed in by guards who risked their jobs. These refugees were registered with some local authority or lived clandestinely with Swiss families. During the war, veritable underground railroads developed, which brought refugees directly to the families that would hide them. And hide them they must, because the Foreigners' Police alternated between amnesties and expulsions. Still, the Foreigners'

Police did not burst into Swiss citizens' homes to take away refugees at gunpoint. Not until August 13, 1942, did the Foreigners' Police order categorically that *all* illegal refugees must be expelled. And as we will see, that order proved to be the beginning of the end of the exclusionary policy.

Official Swiss ambivalence about the refugees was long-standing. In 1938 Rothmund reported to his department head that no refugee would be turned back if he feared for his life: "After all I have heard to this point about the inhuman, cruelly devised treatment to which the Jews of Austria are subjected, I have not been able to bring myself to take on the responsibility of delivering them to their executioners."[6] Still, Rothmund's own policy was one of increasing restriction. Yet Rothmund's occasional leniency was the moral norm for most ordinary Swiss. This caused clashes between border residents and the obedient border guards, and between citizens allied with local officials against the Foreigners' Police. The conflicts increased after Germany's conquest of Europe left Switzerland the only nearby island of safety (Spain and Portugal were willing and even safer, but far away) and as evidence mounted that the incredible, the Holocaust, was actually happening.

One politically virulent sentiment added force to all the factors that are about to be described. By failing to aid the Nazis' victims, the criticism went, the Swiss government was giving aid and comfort to the Nazis, and indeed Nazifying Switzerland. On January 22, 1941, the prestigious daily *Die Nation* printed the following editorial:

Inasmuch as the Zurich Foreigners' Police devotes one line of its Questionnaire B (Application for issuance of Residence Permit) to the applicant's religious affiliation and adds therein the question "Aryan?" one is compelled to inquire what law must be studied in order to establish who is an Aryan? Is Switzerland now covered by the German, the French, the Italian, or the Croatian law on Jewishness?

That is, the bureaucracy's behavior brought upon the Federal Council the worst insult that any Swiss could give another: that he was somehow abetting the Nazis.

In any Christian country, the most subversive of words are St. Peter's statement to the Sanhedrin: "We must obey God rather than men." This is precisely what three hundred Protestant clergymen wrote to the Federal Council on November 19, 1941. They threatened civil disobedience and protested against state interference with the distribution of pro-refugee materials, including Karl Barth's June 1941 lecture "In the name of God, the Almighty." In it, Barth had charged that the Swiss government was intentionally "punishing" the Jews, who, he said, are "opponents and victims of a system whose victory Switzerland must resist to the end with all her strength...."[7] Despite the government's ban on its publication, 16,000 copies were printed privately; available in every kiosk, they sold out in days. Every politically active Swiss knew about it. In late 1939 Rothmund had been able to parry clergymen's criticism by repeating the mantra that the Jews were not in mortal danger and that the clergy had an obligation to civic obedience. But by 1941 the first statement had become incredible. Everyone had heard stories of innocents turned over to the Germans by Swiss authorities and killed. Consequently, the government's claim to loyalty on the basis of an immoral untruth was undermining its own legitimacy. A resistance movement was springing up, and to a growing number of Swiss citizens that movement was the hero while the government was the villain.

From the very first, the Swiss German press had taken literally Himmler's and Hitler's threats to annihilate the Jews (November 1938 and January 1939, respectively). Beginning in 1941 the press began to publish accounts of cattle cars stuffed with Jews heading for death camps in Poland. By early 1942 Swiss observers were privately circulating reports of death transports from occupied Western countries.

In 1941, however, the World Jewish Congress in Geneva discarded the first reports of the Holocaust as incredible. In January 1942 a German Jewish historian who stayed in Germany and survived the Holocaust wrote that the mass killing of Jews had become merely "a very credible rumor." Although he had by March concluded that a "concentration camp is now identical with a death sentence," in January 1943 he still wrote that hard information on the fate of the Jews was difficult to obtain because "the worst measures are concealed from the Aryans."[8]

But in the summer of 1942, when the transports began moving out of France, the Swiss body politic was struck irreversibly. It was then that countless refugees, Jews and Frenchmen fleeing compulsory labor service in the East, physically and undeniably brought the news of the Holocaust. They also brought themselves, which precipitated the crisis.

Swiss authorities redoubled their efforts of 1938 to convince the Allied powers to take the bulk of Jewish refugees who managed to get to Swiss borders. But at the Bermuda conference of 1943, even more than at the Evian conference of 1938, the United States and Britain refused to do anything to mitigate the plight of the Jews, even to bomb railway lines leading to the death camps, going so far as to refrain from mentioning that the Jews were the Nazis' principal victims. (After the conference, Britain allowed—if the Swiss-based Red Cross could arrange it—4,500 Jewish children and five hundred adult guardians to immigrate to Palestine.) By far the greatest number of European Jews—about 350,000, some of whom had first escaped through Switzerland—found haven in Spain and Portugal.

In late July 1942 Heinrich Rothmund wrote to his boss, Justice and Police Minister Eduard von Steiger: "What are we to do? We admit deserters as well as escaped prisoners of war as long as the number of those who cannot proceed further does not rise too high. Political fugitives ... within the Federal Council's 1933 definition are also given asylum. But this 1933 ordinance has virtually become a farce today because every refugee is already in danger of death. . . . Shall we send back only the Jews? This seems to be almost forced upon us."[9] To avoid singling out the Jews, Rothmund, acting on the Federal Council's behalf, issued his August 13 order closing the borders to all refugees and deporting illegals. By August 30, when von Steiger explained that decision in a speech to several hundred young people near Zurich using the metaphor of Switzerland as a lifeboat that was already full, public opinion had already begun to turn him around. Rothmund had already been "twisting slowly, slowly in the wind" for six days, and the lifeboat had begun taking more passengers than ever.

This is what happened. On August 20 Rothmund explained his decision to the leaders of the Swiss Jewish community. The last bit of ambiguity and hope gone, that community withdrew its cooperation. It enlisted Albert Oeri, Liberal member of parliament and eminent publisher of the *Basler Nachrichten*, who telegraphed von Steiger at his vacation home and demanded an immediate hearing. On August 22 Oeri and prominent refugee activist Dr. Gertrude Kurz told von Steiger that the press would link the gruesome details of the Jews' fate with the government's exclusion policy. Unless the government wanted to share responsibility for the fate of the Jews, it had better back off. Von Steiger asked for time. Two day days later, on the 24th, when Rothmund explained government policy to the refugee relief organizations, they threatened to stop all cooperation with the government and to go underground. As the meeting was threatening to end in mutual declarations of enmity, Rothmund was called to the phone. It was von Steiger, explaining that henceforth exceptions would be made, effectively disavowing his faithful bureaucrat.[10] So, von Steiger's "lifeboat" speech was more an effort to minimize and cover his retreat than it was a tightening of policy.

The Federal Council tried to keep the breach small. On September 23 von Steiger explained the toned-down version of government policy to the (powerless) parliament in traditional terms: Our hearts pull us to let in a flood of refugees. The government regrets the instances of innocents' being delivered to their deaths. But if we really use our heads about the country's true interests we will realize that our resources are limited and our capacity to employ these people is even less. Besides, many of the refugees are ungrateful. The government's policy will balance the demands of heart and head.

Support from the three government parties was nuanced. But criticism was withering from Albert Rittmayer, a Radical who proclaimed the government's regrets insincere. While everyone knew the Jews were in danger of death, the council was doing nothing to prevent recurrences of exclusions and expulsions. Swiss resources for refugees, Rittmayer said, were nowhere near the breaking point. The government's policy was unworthy of the Swiss people, and the people would repudiate it.

The opposition piled on, especially the Socialists, and the press shamed the government. With elections scheduled for the following spring, the politicians scrambled for public favor on the side of the refugees.

Although the order to expel illegal immigrants had been rescinded and the government sought to avoid embarrassing incidents, public pressure mounted. In September 1942 dozens of French Jews who had been herded into Paris's Velodrome d'Hiver committed suicide rather than await transport to the Nazi death camps. Swiss headlines screamed, "Death Transports to the East." Official policy could no longer be defended publicly. By 1943 few if any illegal Jewish refugees were being expelled, and more were being accepted legally. In January, 460 Jewish refugees registered in Switzerland; in February, 857; in March, 818; in each of the months of April, May, and June, some 600; in July, more than 700; in August, 900; and in September, more than a thousand. Above these numbers were uncounted illegal entrants. The Swiss lifeboat was turning into a transport ship. Decent, generous officials were no longer penalized. But neither were zealous ones discouraged enough. Not until July 12, 1944, long after the people, "the sovereign," had punished the governing parties in parliamentary elections, did the government officially replace the ludicrous distinction between political, economic, and racial refugees with the reasonable criterion that a refugee is someone who flees in fear of physical persecution.

In the climate of late 1944, as Allied victory loomed, refugee policy turned proactive. The Federal Council was eager to show its goodwill to all refugees, especially Jews. It delegated the serviceable Rothmund to negotiate with Nazi officials to bring to Switzerland some 1,300 Hungarian Jews who had not yet been shipped to the death camps. By this time, Nazi officials were willing to make such deals.

Ultimately, the Federal Council's refugee policy could not have survived an open, running debate in the Swiss parliament. As it was, faulty premises had to be exposed by bloody news. Even that was not enough. The council was finally moved only by civil disobedience and prospects of more, as well as by the erosion of the political base of the councilors' parent political parties. The Federal Council would have been better off without "full powers."

Freedom of the Press

A second set of policies that shifted Swiss public opinion against the Federal Council involved the freedom of the press. The struggle over freedom of the press took place under direct German pressure, but it was a domestic political struggle as well. Those who favored making the press inoffensive to Germany argued that modest censorship was a small price to pay to avoid the risk of enormous harm. The champions of freedom of the press argued that Germany's invasion plans weren't determined by press attacks, and that the Czech and Austrian newspapers' complaisance had not forestalled German invasions of their counties. It was a struggle about the meaning of prudence and true patriotism, and about the role of the Swiss government regarding the press. Nazi Germany was putting all its weight on one side. But the Swiss government did not take the lead on the other side.

The genesis of the problem again dates to World War I, when the army monitored the press to safeguard military secrets, and advocated doing so again in any future European conflict. No one suggested that the government should become responsible for what newspapers said, or that it should dictate content. The idea was to keep irresponsible newspapers from bringing other countries' quarrels onto Swiss heads in wartime. Pressure for censorship, however, began not with any military event but with Hitler's rise to power in January 1933. Almost immediately, the Nazis demanded that the Swiss government direct its press to say certain things and not others. This made nonsense of the Swiss government's fear that the press might create monsters abroad; rather, the problem was that foreign monsters wanted to command the Swiss press. Had the government followed the consequences of its own views it should have thought not about censoring the press, but rather about shielding it from Nazi influence. Instead, it sought ways of making the press less offensive to Germany. This only led to stronger German demands. It took the army until the summer of 1940 to figure out that a free press was essential to maintaining the country's commitment to independence. The Federal Council never quite did discover this. Nevertheless, Swiss civil society proved strong enough to lead the government to shield the press enough for it to play its proper role—though just barely.

Since regimes that live by fraud cannot stand honest reporting, much less counterargument, the Nazi regime controlled Germany's own press. As a result, the German people's demand for Swiss German-language newspapers rose. In the first few months of the regime, most of these were not editorially hostile to Hitler. Markus Feldmann's *Neue Berner Zeitung*, later strongly anti-Nazi, even carried a few compliments. The major Radical and Liberal papers such as the *Neue Zurcher Zeitung* and the *Basler Nachrichten* held their fire because they assumed,

like other European conservatives, that Hitler would be tamed
by German traditionalists. By 1934, after the Swiss German-
language press as a whole had decried the Nazi regime's first
mass murders (the Rohm purge), the Third Reich banned it at
the border, began harassing its reporters, and lodged demands in
Bern that it be curbed.

The Reich demanded that Switzerland, Czechoslovakia, and
Austria enter into reciprocal agreements to keep their newspapers friendly—a kind of journalistic nonaggression pact among
German-speakers. Only Switzerland said no. Foreign Minister
Giuseppe Motta argued that the government could make no
commitments regarding the press because the press was not an
instrument of government.

Alas, the Federal Council did not leave it at that. On March
26, 1934, yielding to an anti-Swiss campaign in Germany's press
as well as to diplomatic pressure, the council issued a decree
authorizing itself to warn, sanction, or seize any newspaper
that endangered good relations with other countries. There
were to be no "violent terms," nor expressions "truly offensive
to foreign [leaders], states, and peoples." The decree reassured
the press that the council had no intention of interfering with
normal reporting or even editorializing—only to curb flagrant
abuses, to protect neutrality, and to avoid provoking war.
Although everyone realized that the difference between normal journalism and abuse is subjective, no major journalist
objected, perhaps because of faith in the country's leadership.
When Motta explained in 1938 that "neutrality is a doctrine
of states and not of individuals, nevertheless measure and reflection are incumbent on individuals," few doubted he meant to
impose anything more than the rule of reason.

Three problems, however, bedeviled government policy. First, accurately describing the Nazi regime required harsh words. Second, the notion of "offensive" language gave the "offended" party the right to define the bounds of propriety and ban any expression whatever. The Nazis used this pretense to try imposing on Switzerland what they called a "cultural *Anschluss.*" Third, the order contradicted, *prima facie,* freedom of the press. Whenever government controls any kind of expression, it implicitly approves what it does not penalize.[11] Nevertheless, the Swiss government did assert Switzerland's freedom of the press for anti-Nazi Jewish emigrés. In 1935 the French-based emigré journalist Berthold Jacob Salomon was kidnapped by German agents in Basel and taken to Germany for trial. Swiss police caught one of the kidnappers, and Switzerland pushed the matter so vehemently that Hitler ended up freeing Salomon.

Prior to the war, politicians and bureaucrats limited themselves to informal admonitions to the press to take it easy on Hitler and Mussolini. These were uniformly ignored. In 1938, when the entire press raged against the Munich sellout of Czechoslovakia, the Swiss government slapped the wrist of one (foreign-financed) paper. At war's outbreak, however, the Federal Council directed the army's Division of Press and Radio to monitor the media, distribute guidance, hand out warnings, and impose sanctions, including suspension of the right to publish.

Editors chose between fighting the censors, approving bland commentaries, or simply quoting from the press releases of the Axis and the Allies.[12] For example, on the morning of May 10, 1940, when Germany attacked France, the Division of Press and Radio allowed the Swiss media to report noises that sounded like shooting as well as troop movement north of Basel. How to characterize what happened to Norway? An attack. It was important to point out that a small country's borders had been violated by a great power. But value judgments were judged imprudent. What about Belgium? Here the division allowed the word "aggression." After all, Belgium enjoyed the same status in international law as Switzerland, and to have said less would have shown undue lack of concern for Switzerland's own status. The point was to walk a fine line between telling the truth and angering Germany. The army soon realized that curbing the press meant morally disarming the country—so much so that it felt it necessary to set up its own capillary system of information for civilians. In mid-1940 the army began to beg the Federal Council to take censorship off its shoulders. It became a government function on January 1, 1942.

The division was headed by high-quality people. The first chief was a federal judge on army duty; an advisory committee of prominent journalists acted as a watchdog on the censors. The division also had strict orders not to interfere on debates of domestic issues. But the bureaucracy contained the usual quota of low-level, ham-handed functionaries. Also, during the war there were few if any purely domestic matters. The domestic question *par excellence* was whether the country should adapt itself to the New European Order or resist.

Germany's direct approach backfired. In 1937 and 1938 the Reich had expelled the correspondents of the leading Swiss German dailies, hoping to ruin their careers and make their successors more pliant. Instead they had become heroes. On June 14, 1940, German press attaché Georg Trump informed his contact in the Swiss Foreign Ministry that the editors of these newspapers were obstacles to good relations and demanded that they be replaced. Here is the memorandum of conversation:

Mr. Trump told me that after the separate peace with France certain Swiss newspapers will cease to exist in their current form. He gave the example of the *National Zeitung*. Others will have to change their editorial management. Thus the *Bund* will have to dispense with the services of Mr. Schurch. I asked him how the changes would be brought about. The answer is very simple, he said: From that moment, Europe will only have two press agencies: the DNB [*Deutsches Nachrichten Büro*] and the *Stefani* [Italian agency]. The newspapers who do not stay in rank will no longer receive the services of these agencies and thus will no longer be able to exist.[13]

Trump then took his demand to fire Schurch to the owner of *Der Bund*, Fritz Pochon, and mentioned that Germany would be making similar demands on the *Neue Zurcher Zeitung*, the *Basler Nachrichten*, and the Swiss wire service. Far from throwing the German diplomat out of his office, Pochon seriously considered complying. He talked things over with other owners and editors as well as with the Swiss Foreign Ministry. Nearly a month later, he wrote to Foreign Minister Pilet Golaz that he and the press would resist. Thenceforth, the Swiss press rejected direct German pressure.

What about the government's role in this? If government has any role, it is to stand between its own citizens and foreign governments. Pilet Golaz should have admonished Herr Trump after his first demarche, and expelled him after the second. Upon receipt of Pochon's first call, President Pilet Golaz should have asked him to cease all communication with German officials, because their request was the business of the state. Instead, the Swiss state countenanced the possibility that some of its own citizens would determine the employment of others based on the demands of a foreign government. Thus the Swiss state let the Swiss press stand alone before the power of triumphant Germany.

Note that Germany's demand to fire editors and close newspapers came also from Nazi sympathizers in Switzerland. It was included on the list of demands the pro-Nazi National Frontists presented to Pilet Golaz on September 10, 1940; it was part of a petition that 173 people, some of them prominent personalities, presented to the Federal Council; and it was one of the main points in the complaint Colonel Gustav Daniker filed in May 1941.

Still, the only newspapers the Swiss government ever closed down were those of Nazi supporters. Nor will it do to allege that the final banning of *Die Front* and *Der Grenzbote* in 1943 (despite the violent objections of Herr Trump) was due to the turning tide of war. The Federal Council had also banned the soft-on-Nazism *Neue Basler Zeitung* in 1939 and lesser frontist publications even in the grim year of 1940. But never did the government close down a patriotic anti-Nazi paper, regardless of Germany's threats. The Federal Council was clearly afraid of Germany, but it also feared the wrath of anti-Nazi Swiss.

Perhaps the strongest challenge from the anti-Nazi side came from the same quarter as the challenge on refugee policy: Christian activists. The mechanism for controlling the press, like the one for implementing refugee policy, relied heavily on the cooperation of private organizations appointed to serve on the advisory board. This is how modern big government works everywhere: Private organizations exchange their cooperation with government policy for a voice in the formulation of policy and above all for a certain indulgence in the application of policy in their own regard. One of the private organizations that the government thought it necessary to appoint to its "liaison service for press questions" was the *Evangelischer Pressdienst* (Protestant press service). On October 28, 1941, the service's director, Roger Frey, resigned from the board, charging that the government was forbidding Christians from doing their duty of calling things by their name. Nazism was evil, and the government was trying to force Christians into silent complicity with it. The Protestant churches had already circumvented the government by printing and distributing Karl Barth's famous lecture, and they could do it again. The government could not afford to have substantial numbers of respected, mainstream citizens withdraw their cooperation. What if the big papers, which also chafed under censorship, followed suit? How many journalists could the government afford to arrest? Consequently, press guidelines eased. So in the end, the boundaries of the press control system were set by civil society itself.

Civil society's preferences were never in doubt. But the political consequences of these preferences certainly were. In 1940 the weightiest political issue for the press was to come to terms with the apparently permanent defeat of democracy and liberalism as well as of Britain and France. How would Switzerland fit into the New Europe? What changes would have to be made? The French language press was most prone to adopt the language of the Pétain regime in Vichy. Words like "work," "family," and "authority" were bandied about, but no one would reapply them to Swiss politics with any precision. The German language press tried to find an alternative to democracy and liberalism in ancient, mythical Swiss traditions. But it did not discuss why any Swiss should want such things. What would they mean in terms of practical changes to the constitution and the laws? And would any of these changes be enough to appease the Germans? The government played next to no role in this debate.

Much as the Swiss government lacked courage and insight, it accepted pushes from the right side and not from the wrong. It did little good, but it did not do much harm, and did not prevent the better elements in Swiss society from prevailing.

Accommodation vs. Resistance

If the struggle between accommodation and resistance had been merely a matter of ideological preferences, there would have been no contest. Even at the depths of national despair in the early summer of 1940, the small number of people who actually wanted to accommodate the Germans were able to elicit in their fellow citizens resignation at most. The biggest advocates of accommodation were businessmen with foreign contracts, labor unions, and bureaucrats concerned about unemployment. But note that the purpose of the Federal Council's economic concessions was to hold the domestic front *politically*. In this regard, it is strange that the government, and especially Pilet Golaz, are ordinarily thought of as having made political concessions in domestic policy. They did not.

Marcel Pilet Golaz, from the Francophone heartland of Vaud, was a brilliant, haughty technocrat who made his mark as minister of the country's excellent railroad network between 1930 and 1940. His pride in his own judgment and his tendency to regard the objects of public policy as his personal property only increased when he took over the Foreign Ministry and the presidency for the crucial year of 1940. He kept his own counsel, and was cold and bureaucratic. His sentiments for the *boches*, the Germans, were no more positive than those of the majority of French-speakers. He thought Nazi Germany had already won the war, and was convinced that getting the best out of any given balance of power was a technical task, and that he knew how to handle it.

The standard sentiment of the Swiss *Romands* about France's defeat was expressed by Denis de Rougemont's 1940 account of Paris under the Germans. Physically untouched, the city had become a soulless cemetery of masonry, he wrote. Paris under "the invader" (de Rougemont never named Hitler or Germany) had lost what gave life worth and meaning. The "war chieftain" who would cruise the world's most famous streets might think he was possessing her, but he was only raping a dead body. Any regular fellow could fulfill himself on a June evening by watching the sun set over Saint Germain des Pres, by contemplating the places where so much of mankind's wisdom and misery had passed—but the conquerors could have none of that. These savages just didn't understand. And so, concluded de Rougemont, "forgive them, for they know not what they do."[14] The article did not dispute Germany's victory over France, raise doubts about the Reich's ultimate victory in the war, or suggest that anyone resist. It just found the whole thing surpassingly sad. The Swiss censors gave the *Gazette de Lausanne* trouble for accusing a foreign head of state of necrophilia.

Eight days later, when President Pilet Golaz spoke to the nation after France's surrender, his speech was as sad as de Rougemont's article. But speaking on behalf of the Federal Council (to which he had not submitted the text), Pilet Golaz said he was obliged not just to talk, but also "to provide, to decide, to act." In his cleverness, he chose to spell out only one policy and to leave the rest as fuzzy as possible. That policy was to "surmount every obstacle" in order to "assure to all—and it is a primordial duty—the bread that nourishes the body and the work that comforts the soul." To this end he told the Swiss people to forget political argumentation, to obey the Federal Council even when they did not like it; he warned that the council would not be able to explain what it was doing. The rest of the speech was a series of regrets for a world that had been swept away, and commiseration with the Swiss people for a future life that would be worse in every way. The people would have to work harder for less, give up large hopes to ensure the minimum, forget humanitarianism, think only about fulfilling their immediate duties, and not gripe. It was a lot like President Jimmy Carter's disastrous 1979 speech to the American people in which he told Americans to accept an age of more limited horizons, to look wistfully on past grandeur, to learn to like government power, and to blame themselves for any feelings of "malaise."

Insofar as the speech was an exercise in interest-group politics, it was a rousing success. The Socialist press hailed its commitment to full employment no matter what, and industrialists expressed satisfaction. The Germans liked it. But the speech energized no one, gave no confidence in the future, and opened the door to suspicions that the Federal Council might be selling out to the Germans. Then, shortly thereafter, when news spread that Pilet Golaz had granted an audience to three representatives of the pro-Nazi National Front, those suspicions came to dominate Swiss politics and to ruin his career.

But Pilet Golaz did not promise the National Front anything. He did not even issue a polite joint communiqué. Rather, the National Front issued its own statement, which tacitly suggested that the president had negotiated with the Front rather than just listened to its demands. For the most part, these demands did not sound so different from government policy. In foreign affairs, Switzerland should show a "loyal friendship" with the victorious powers. Domestically, economic policy should aim at "bread and work for all," doing away with political parties and establishing a "responsible" executive capable of tough decisions. As regards religion, the Frontists made no mention of the Jews and insisted only that religion be pushed out of politics. In sum, the content was not shocking.[15] Nor, from an objective standpoint, was anything wrong with the president's meeting with law-abiding citizens to discuss their ideas. Moreover, for Pilet Golaz, meeting with the Frontists behind closed doors was a way of giving the Germans cheap satisfaction. There is no evidence that he planned to give them, or the Germans, anything. And in fact he did not give them anything. Within three months he had put the Front out of business and many of its operatives in jail.

Swiss public opinion nevertheless was shocked by the meeting, as it had been by Pilet Golaz's returning the remains of German aircraft shot down during the battle of France to Germany and issuing a thinly veiled apology. Public opinion labeled Pilet Golaz an accommodationist. He was too proud to defend himself, and although the Federal Council held on to him for four more years, his image was fixed for the worse in the summer of 1940. He immediately became a liability to his colleagues in domestic politics. As time showed that Pilet Golaz's judgment about the war had erred on the side of pessimism, he became a symbol of his country's subservience to the Germans. His replacement, Max Petitpierre, was welcome both to the Swiss and to the Allies, having been chief of the watchmakers' Chamber of Commerce, and hence the man in charge of supplying the exports most prized by the Allies.

Yet Pilet Golaz's and the council's technocratic policies were defensible. First among them was a plan to lessen the country's dependence on Germany for food. During the nineteenth century Swiss agriculture had followed its natural comparative advantage and concentrated on the export of cheese, other milk products such as chocolate, and then tinned meat. Switzerland imported most of its grain, oils, and fibers. In 1940, with normal international trade cut off, Switzerland would have eaten only at the Reich's pleasure had not the council adopted the radical plan of agronomist Friedrich Traugott Wahlen—to plant every plantable square meter in the country, including soccer fields, public gardens, and private yards. This meant reducing the nation's cattle by about a third, and milk production even more. It also meant drafting men, women, and children from the cities for forced labor on the land, as well as for felling trees and making charcoal. In return, the production of grains doubled, potatoes nearly tripled, and oilseeds were up by a factor of fifty. Switzerland even exported some food. The Swiss did suffer rationing, although the minimum ration never went below 2,400 calories, most qualified for more, the rural population was practically exempt, and many if not most people augmented their rations with food they grew or purchased privately in the countryside. So, the Federal Council's authoritarianism produced better nutrition than anywhere in continental Europe or Britain.

As for industrial workers, they certainly did not lack jobs throughout the war. But as Pilet Golaz had intimated in his speech, life turned out worse. Prices rose quickly, by 60 percent, while wages rose slowly, by only half that amount. But it was not the Federal Council's fault. The next chapter will show that the decrease in purchasing power was due to the fact that the Axis's military encirclement had left Swiss industry with only one customer, one that had nearly absolute power to set the sales list and the terms of trade—at least during the first thirty months of the war. Yet the politically significant fact is that the Federal Council did not tell the people that they were being exploited by a rapacious Reich. The council judged, probably correctly, that the people were already all too prepared to vent their anti-German feelings, and that their doing so would have done no good and possibly much harm.

Pilet Golaz had said, after all, that the council would not be able to explain all its actions. So, for want of the facts, by the end of the war workers' circles were abuzz with rumors that the difference between the value of their work and the pittances they received must somehow have enriched the Swiss elites. No. The lion's share of the difference was fed to the Reich's war machine, and the rest went to build the Swiss army. The people also resented the government's authoritarianism. When Wahlen suggested that the autarkic agricultural system be retained after the war, public reaction was scornful. One can understand the bitter point of view of Pilet Golaz and his colleagues: Their competence had delivered food, work, and safety—the best that circumstances would allow—and still the people were ungrateful.

The calculations that underlay the council's attitude were indeed "realistic." Why in 1940–1941 should a responsible government not have listened to the accommodationists' logical argument—namely, that the New Europe was being made whether tiny Switzerland liked it or not, and that the essence of policy competence lay in finding some role for Switzerland with as little pain as possible? The accommodationists argued that the resisters were offering blood, sweat, and tears before a catastrophic defeat and, afterward, much worse. By contrast, competent policy would aim at trading concessions in foreign policy and economics for internal political freedom. The resisters, for their part, argued that the Nazis, if victorious, would never grant Switzerland internal independence except if forced to by Swiss military deterrence. That, too, was obvious. They hoped for but did not bet on the Allies' victory. Instead, perhaps foolishly, they bet that if the Swiss people bolstered their fighting spirit they would be able to muster military deterrence. The council acknowledged both sets of arguments.

Did the council "Finlandize" Switzerland? When the Soviet Union attacked Finland in the winter of 1940, everyone in Switzerland identified with the Finns. They cheered Finland's glorious defense of the Mannerheim Line, as well as its heroic guerrilla warfare, and were enormously saddened by Finland's final ordeal—cession of territory, a heavy indemnity, as well as loss of control over domestic and foreign policy (but, thank God, not occupation). Avoiding Finland's fate was a very hot topic. Fortunately for the Swiss, because the Reich never demanded of Switzerland as much as the Soviets had demanded of Finland, the confrontation never came to blows. In foreign policy the Reich demanded silence rather than support. Not too bad. In economics, the tribute demanded was not intolerable. And as regards domestic policy, the Nazis were content enough to swallow their failures to interfere. So the Finlandization of Switzerland's foreign policy reached its (relatively low) peak in July 1940, and three years later was in rapid decline. Domestically, Finlandization never really occurred, though the threat was almost always present.

That threat of Finlandization came from the fact that the council's technical, economic, interest-group approach to politics did nothing to inspire the Swiss people to be themselves and defend themselves. The Federal Council's leaders—Pilet Golaz, Finance Minister Walter Stampfli, and Karl Kobelt—were deaf to the appeals of the heart, to the deepest aspirations of their countrymen. It did not occur to them that they should occupy themselves with what President George Bush later called "the vision thing." And so the Swiss people gave their hearts to the resisters.

The resisters did not prevail by being what we call "policy wonks." One of the two principal resisters' organizations, the minuscule Gotthard League, issued a manifesto on domestic policy whose welfare statism was not all that different from government policy nor even from that of the pro-Nazi fronts. The other, the National Resistance Action (*Aktion Nationaler Widerstand*), spoke more in terms of traditional Swiss economic liberalism. But that was not the point. Rather, both organizations put out one simple, appealing message: The Switzerland we have known is good. Nazism is bad. Let us do everything in our power to preserve our way of life into the future.

Of course the Nazis helped the resisters' cause immeasurably. By mid-1941 the image of an efficient, if authoritarian, "New Europe" had been canceled out by the nightmarish reality of compulsion and camps. The accommodationists had no positive theme to sell, and they did not even try hard to sell it. No one could feel good about himself by agreeing with the accommodationists. By contrast, the resisters touted on the one hand the cacotopia of Nazism, and on the other the hope that, with noble resolution (not to mention Allied victory), good old Switzerland might come back.

The Federal Council was jealous of General Guisan. Everywhere he went, people crowded around him, cheered him, prayed and wept for him, wanted him to touch their children. His car could hardly traverse a village without setting off a celebration. None of the councilors elicited any positive popular feeling at all. Exasperated, the president for 1943, Finance Minister Walter Stampfli, had a placard affixed to his car identifying him in three languages as the president of the confederation. This elicited either laughter or resentment.

What did Guisan have that the technically competent federal councilors didn't? When his country's fate looked darkest, he put himself at the head of the cause of hope, against new evils, and for the restoration of all good, familiar things. And he was lucky. That's all.

CHAPTER 4

Economics

"Vae Victis!"

—Brennus

BESIEGED IN THEIR CAPITOL by Brennus's barbarians from the north, the Romans had struck a bargain—so many measures of gold for lifting the siege. But as the gold was being weighed out, the Romans complained that the scales were fraudulent. Brennus's reply, "Woe to the vanquished," is usually translated as "To the victor belong the spoils." To show that power trumps agreements, Brennus tossed his sword onto the balance. Legend has it that just then Furius Camillus (whose family name, then as now, implies a powerful emotion) appeared with the Roman army and declared, sword in hand, "Not with gold is the fatherland ransomed, but with iron." Since Camillus beat Brennus, the scales' accuracy was irrelevant. Had the battle gone the other way, it still would have been irrelevant: Brennus and the furious Roman agreed on one thing—the weight of gold matters less than the weight of swords.

Almost two-and-a-half millennia later, when the Swiss were besieged by the barbarian from the north and his Roman camp follower, they bargained nonstop about credit, about the terms of their merchandise trade, as well as about the uses to which the besiegers wanted to put the Swiss currency. In this respect, keep in mind Montesquieu's dictum on economics: "Commerce is the profession of equals"—that is, true economic transactions take place when buyers and sellers are influenced only by the value they put on the goods exchanged. When one of the parties throws a sword into the balance, the relationship ceases to be economic. During the Second World War, both the Germans and the Swiss threw swords into their bargains. Those swords, of course, were of vastly different sizes at various times, and a third set of swords was floating around—that of the barbarians' main enemies, the British and the Americans. So determined were these enemies to defeat the barbarians that they made demands on the Swiss regarding merchandise and currency not so different from those that the barbarians themselves were making. Obviously, the Swiss tried to balance the two sets of demands in their own interest.

Since time immemorial, small nations have been physically surrounded or otherwise importuned by larger ones at war with one another. Thucydides' magisterial *Peloponnesian War* describes a dozen instances of negotiations that have occurred innumerable times in history. The small, would-be neutrals hear from both overwhelming armies: We have nothing against you. We really like you. We are fighting for our lives against our mortal enemies. If you really think about it, they are your mortal enemies, too. So we are really fighting your fight. You should be grateful. In these desperate days, we must have your help. It would be nice if you could make war on our enemy directly. If you cannot, we ask you at least to give us access to your economy, and above all not to trade with the enemy. We would like to pay you for the goods we want from you. But just now, for a variety of reasons that you must understand, we can't come up with the cash, and you must accept our IOU. You trust us, don't you? If you do as we say, you prove your real neutrality. If you insist on trading with the enemy, we will be immediately compelled to isolate you economically from our side, and to cut off the flow of so many products on which your livelihood depends. We might even devastate your crops. After we win, we will treat you like an enemy. So, regardless of what happens in the long run, woe to you if you don't help us now. And mega woes to you if you bet wrong on the eventual winner.

To this, the small would-be neutrals reply: We sympathize with you, trust you, agree that your enemies are dastardly, and would like nothing better than to take your IOUs in exchange for uninterrupted commerce and being left alone (that is, to pay you ransom). But we have a problem. Your enemies are making the same demands on us that you are making. If we accede to your demands, they will hurt us. We fear them, and you cannot protect us against them. Also, despite your declarations of friendship, your threats are fearsome, too. We cannot satisfy you both. So we propose to both you and your enemies that our economic dealings with you both be equally free and friendly.

"No dice!" both sides always answer. Both sides cite the enemy's repugnance. Both say that the necessity to defeat the enemy makes it necessary to hurt those who won't cooperate.

Therefore, Thucydides shows, comparative fear—which side can do most harm—overrides the small neutrals' other calculations. But since the great power that can do us most harm now may not be the one that can do it later, there is an inherent conflict between short- and long-term fears. And even if we judge correctly that the side to be feared least now is to be feared most in the long term, we must still somehow survive the short term. And so Thucydides gives us the little Sicilian city of Camarina as an example of prudence. Beset by both Syracuse and Athens, Camarina decided to appease them both as best it could, but to lean to Syracuse—the power it liked least, but that could do Camarina the most harm because it was physically closest. It helped Camarina's reputation for good judgment that Athens lost the war.

The lesson for the major powers who want economic favors from small neutrals (and for the neutrals themselves) is then twofold. For the great power: First, squeeze the goose that lays the eggs you want, but neither kill it nor drive it to the enemy. Your demands at any given time must be such that the small power's compliance with them will not impair its capacity to meet future demands, nor be so onerous that its immediate interest will be to work even more closely with the enemy. Second, unless forced by dire need, keep foremost in mind what you want from the small neutral *after* the war. For the small neutral, the rules are reversed: First, do just enough to avoid invasion or sanctions. Manage the appeasement of both sides' demands to do as little damage as possible to the domestic economy. Second, do not let national policy sway to either side for the sake of domestic interest groups that have ties to either side, and make sure that everyone in the country understands the balance between the economic actions forced on you at any given time and your political preferences.

In the present case, both the Reich and the Allies squeezed Switzerland as hard as the balance of power allowed. As for the Swiss Federal Council, its response to the pressures of both sides was about as proportionate to the balance of power as possible—but only *ex post facto*, and not as a result of conscious planning. Moreover, it managed this double appeasement while safeguarding the structural integrity of economy and currency—a solid technical feat. But the economic management was swayed by interest groups whose prosperity depended on the warring powers, and certainly did not reflect a coherent understanding of the balance between fears of present harm and hopes for the future.

To begin with, consider the meaning of economic warfare in World War II for both the Reich and the Anglo-American Allies. Then glance at Switzerland's international economic situation before the war, and how that was affected by the Anglo-American blockade and the German counterblockade. And finally look at three economic battlefields: the competition for Swiss merchandise and credit, the struggle for the use of the Swiss franc, and the questions surrounding the use of Swiss economic institutions as a "safe haven" for the assets of innocents and Nazis. Regarding each of these struggles, did each side do the best for itself that circumstances allowed?

The economics of Switzerland are covered by a thick blanket of conspiracy literature. Some of it—Werner Rings's *Nazi Gold*—has become very influential.

Economic Warfare and the Neutrals, 1939–1945

In the European theater, both sides deemed the economic factor decisive. Though economic warfare turned out to be less important than expected, both waged it doggedly. Both sides believed that the Great War had been decided by an imbalance in industrial production, and that the Allied blockade had hurt Germany more than any battle had. British and American experts believed that Germany lacked the resources to fight another major war. Of the thirty-four materials then judged essential to modern war, Germany had only one aplenty, coal. Germany has almost no iron and no petroleum. How could anyone fight a war without *them*? Never mind the ferrous alloys, rubber, bauxite, fats, nitrates, and so on. That explains in part the West's disbelief that Hitler's bluster meant war.

The Germans, meanwhile, were so aware of their economic deficiencies that they stockpiled strategic materials, developed *ersatz* products, and planned lightning-short military campaigns, the *Blitzkrieg*. They also planned to conquer the European continent, to exploit its resources fully, and to deny them to the enemy. Britain, joined by the United States, necessarily countered with the classic sea-power strategy: Sweep enemy commerce from the seas. Bring to bear the resources of the world, the oil of the Middle East and Texas, the rubber of the Indies, the alloys of South Africa, and all the rest, to build navies and air forces that would isolate the continent, pound it, wait for continental conflicts to weaken it, and eventually allow seaborne armies to defeat those of the land powers.

In short, the Germans sought to exploit the continent economically, while the Allies blockaded and bombed to diminish it.

As for neutral countries, the Germans planned straightforward plunder and exploitation, limited only by the realization that it makes no sense to overextend armies to get things that may be had less expensively. Thus Germany never invaded Romania, and instead got all it wanted from it—precious petrol—through a combination of military intimidation, money, and ideological affinity. Money and intimidation were enough to get Swedish iron ore and timber. But from Spain, the Reich got only trade goods at competitive prices, despite presumed ideological affinity, and the *Wehrmacht* at the border. If Hitler was going to get Spain's strategic prize, access to Gibraltar, Nazi Germany must either defeat Spanish as well as

British troops or submit to intentionally impossible Spanish demands.

The Allies' approach to the European neutrals was to assume that the Reich had great influence over their economies and *therefore that any shipload of anything they allowed to land on the continent could get to the Germans or could free up resources that would help the Germans.* Already in 1917 the Allies had thrown out the centuries-old international law, most recently refined by the Hague Convention of 1907, by which belligerents could block-ade only enemies and could prevent neutrals from delivering to them only "absolute contraband"—namely, weapons of war. Restrictions on neutral trade of each and every item that might or might not help a belligerent, "conditional contraband," would have to be justified to international courts. Trade in purely civilian goods was to be unrestricted. But by 1917 the Allies had become convinced that the fungibility of resources in modern war made contraband of everything that might be use-ful to the enemy, including children's toys. So the United States, which in the eighteenth and nineteenth centuries had been primarily responsible for expanding the international law con-cept of neutral rights to trade, joined Great Britain in a new blockade system that started from the assumption that there was no such thing as a neutral right to trade: *Nothing whatsoever would be allowed to cross the seas to any country on the European continent unless the shipment had been previously approved by the American and British offices of economic warfare.* These offices deter-mined just what the European neutrals would be allowed to receive from the world, and authorized each shipment with a navigation certificate, or *"navicert."* Allied agents in every port made sure that no unauthorized ship sailed. If any tried, the Allied agents would report it to the Allied navies for sinking or seizure. Allied economic warfare offices would also judge how much of what the neutrals shipped to the world might ultimately produce revenue for the enemy. Hence the Allies allowed each European neutral country to export only its quota of "enemy content."

The Germans, for their part, imposed a counterblockade. The Reich's economic warriors granted *Geleitscheine* to the neutrals whose access to the sea they controlled—certificates for exports that Germans judged would not help the Allies.

Note the circular justification for such extremism: In both World Wars, all the belligerent governments worked hard to eliminate domestic production, as well as imports from neutral countries, of anything that was not militarily useful. Since the protagonists in the world wars were the biggest and richest countries, the world market for nonmilitary goods well nigh collapsed. Even without the blockades and counterblockades, the neutrals found that all of the belligerents canceled contracts for delivery of purely civilian goods, except of course food, medicine, and other civilian supplies that were also useful for military purposes. Consequently, the neutrals had either to become war suppliers or to get largely out of the international merchandise trade.

There were five European neutrals, practically divided into two-and-a-half categories. Portugal, Spain, and Turkey were not surrounded by the Axis, and were more or less freely accessible to the Allies by sea. Switzerland was an inland island surrounded by the Axis. Sweden was in between; it had access to the seas, but for most of the war those seas were dominated by German aircraft and minefields.

With respect to Portugal, Spain, and Turkey, the Axis's and the Allies' power was balanced. The Germans and the Allies could pressure these three countries in roughly the same economic ways, by denying them shipments from, or market access to, the areas the great powers controlled. But while the Germans could deny them access only to Occupied Europe's products, the Allies could cut them off from the world. Nor had the Germans any monopoly on anything these neutrals needed. So, because the broad, non-European world had more goods and more markets to offer than did German-controlled Europe, the Allies always had more strictly economic influence in these three countries. As a result, the Germans offered the Spanish, Portuguese, and Turks competitive prices for their tungsten, chrome, dried fruits, and oils. But these neutrals knew that if they were to buy something to eat or to burn with that money, they would have to do it overseas—and for that they would need *navicerts* from the Anglo-American economic warriors. In addition to money, the Germans initially offered a place in the New Europe, and of course lots of fear. But the image of the former faded within a year, and the latter was gone by 1943. The Allies would urge these neutrals to curtail their trade with the Axis and would emphasize the point by restricting their *navicerts*. When the Allies began to add fear to their mix of economic incentives, these neutrals' neutrality disappeared. In 1944 Turkey declared war on Germany after long collaboration with the Allies, Portugal gave the Allies base rights in the Azores (*finis* to Germany's chances in the Battle of the Atlantic), and maligned Spain reminded the Allies that they had been able to use the Mediterranean only because Spain had protected Gibraltar's northern approach. All three nations had a claim for having been on the Allied side all along!

But Sweden, and above all Switzerland, were within the German counterblockade. Because they could receive nothing of which the Germans did not approve, the Germans had a monopoly on every import they needed, even on overseas imports. Even if the Allies granted unlimited *navicerts*, the Germans would still allow in only what *they* wanted the Swedes or Swiss to have. Hence for the Germans, putting the Swiss economy to work for the Reich was child's play. Just cut off the coal and Swiss industry would stop. People would be out of work. They would freeze. Delay food imports, and they would go hungry. Don't give them contracts and *Geleitscheine*, and their exports would stop and they would run out of money. Want to play with the Swiss currency? Sell gold on the Swiss domestic market to foreigners. This would drive down the price of the metal backing the franc, forcing the government to issue gold-convertible francs to buy gold to keep up its value. Meanwhile the holders of these francs will be trading them in for Swiss government gold. Since you would not allow the Swiss to export what the rest of the world wanted, the Swiss would have to choose between producing what *you* wanted for *you*, or nothing at all.

Next to this array, the Allies' economic weapons were few and could easily become counterproductive. The Allies could no more help Switzerland economically than they could militarily. Prior to the war Great Britain had sold Switzerland some 300,000 tons of coal per year, as against Germany's 1.8 million. The British would have been delighted to make up any quantity of coal that the Germans might refuse to sell—provided they could buy what they wanted on the Swiss market. But once the German counterblockade was in place, the Allies could neither supply coal to Switzerland nor count on any Swiss deliveries. Consequently, when the Allies made requests of the Swiss, they were not necessarily dealing with people capable of fulfilling them. The Allies and the Swiss might make a deal for quantities of jewel bearings, but the Germans would not allow the trade to pass. Allied threats against the Swiss failed for the same reason: When the Allies asked the Swiss not to produce so many arms for the Reich, or asked the Swedes not to send the Reich so much iron ore, and made their point by restricting *navicerts*, these neutrals expressed genuine sorrow but noted that they couldn't live without German coal and steel deliveries. That is why Allied economic warriors did not press their points too far with the Swedes, and especially with the Swiss.

Through the war the Reich got about 1.35 billion Swiss francs' worth of war goods from Switzerland (out of some 2.5 billion in total deliveries). This included machine tools especially useful for producing tanks and airplanes, timing devices, and more. Yet this war materiel amounted to only about 0.6 percent of the Reich's total military procurement of 210 billion reichsmarks—not a lot. But then again, the Reich "paid" for most of this merchandise with reichsmarks credits in Berlin's Reichsbank, which no rational person expected would ever be redeemed.

Meanwhile, the Allies, and the "dollar zone" of Latin America, absorbed a total of about 1.6 billion francs' worth of Swiss exports. Some of these exports were the high-tech jewel bearings for aircraft navigation, on which the Swiss had something of a world monopoly. After 1941 the jewel bearings had to be smuggled through German-controlled territory. But about three-fourths of Swiss wartime exports to the Allies were watches. These went exclusively to the military, freeing Allied watch factories for other war production. This amounted to a smaller percentage of Anglo-American military procurement, but it too was paid for with a kind of credit—gold that could not be removed from the New York Federal Reserve Bank until after postwar negotiations.

All told, Swiss merchandise made no real difference to the outcome of the war. But both the Axis and the Allies wanted Swiss francs, and wound up with roughly 3 billion of them. The Germans paid for them in gold, delivered in Bern. The Allies paid for them in gold, locked up in New York. For the Allies, the francs were very useful. For the Reich, they were a vital means of obtaining specialty metals and oil.

Merchandise Trade Before and During the Blockades

Before the war international merchandise trade directly accounted for fully 20 percent of the Swiss economy. (By comparison, the figure was under 3 percent for the United States.) That trade was spread widely. In 1938, 15.7 percent of Swiss exports went to Germany, while 17.1 percent went to France and the border countries Belgium, the Netherlands, and Luxembourg. Britain took 11.2 percent, the United States and Canada 8.1 percent, and such places as Argentina, Japan, and India about 3 percent each. The rest was spread evenly throughout the world.[1] Roughly the same was true of imports. Switzerland, however, ran a perpetual, large merchandise trade deficit. This was more than made up for by income from Swiss investments around the world, notably in the U.S., from tourism, and from the sale to foreigners of patents and services such as banking and insurance. The Swiss economy was also perhaps the world's most open, having resisted some of the global trends of the 1930s toward exchange controls and blatant import quotas. Its currency was formally convertible to gold by central banks, and informally by private parties, since the Swiss gold market was free and the National Bank was statutorily required to maintain the value of the franc between 190 and 215 grains of gold. Hence, of all the world's economies, Switzerland's was perhaps the most vulnerable to disruption by war.

When Britain imposed its blockade of 1939, it leisurely negotiated with Switzerland a War Trade Agreement. Britain, mistress of the seas, was in a position to stop Swiss overseas commerce, but not to prevent Germany from making up much of the loss. Britain therefore agreed to grant *navicerts* virtually on demand so long as the Swiss did not increase the percentage of trade with the Reich above prewar levels. Britain also agreed to the concept of "compensation goods"—Swiss exports to Germany manufactured with materials let through the blockade, in exchange for Swiss exports to Britain manufactured with raw materials imported from Germany. This was a good deal for both the Allies and the Swiss, and as good a deal as Germany might have expected.

In 1939–1940 Britain, France, Belgium, and the Netherlands placed 540 million francs' worth of military orders in Switzerland, while the total for German war industries was 88 million. But even that understates the imbalance, because most of Germany's orders went to divisions of German companies that had been established in Switzerland after World War I to evade the arms-control provisions of the Versailles Treaty.[2] In short, Switzerland was working for the Allied war effort, and for cash.

Germany was in no position to object, because it was in no position to overcome Swiss preferences with more cash or, more important, to interfere with Swiss commerce. Yes, the Rhine was one of Switzerland's windows on the world, and Germany controlled it. But the French port of Marseilles and the Italian port of Genoa were at least as important to Swiss commerce as the ports of the lower Rhine. So, on April 25,

1940, Switzerland and Britain signed the accord. Switzerland then began negotiating a parallel agreement with the Reich. The German negotiators did not demand that Switzerland abrogate the accord with Britain, and did not seek a monopoly on Swiss trade.

As France was falling, however, Germany's position hardened. On June 18, 1940, the Reich cut coal deliveries to Switzerland to zero, and the Swiss economy became thoroughly unbalanced. Force set the terms of trade.

In the 1930s the dictatorships had already begun to treat trade as an instrument of conflict. Prior to World War I, any company in a given European country that wanted to buy goods abroad would use domestic currency or gold to buy the foreign currency needed to pay the seller. But since the postwar dictatorships wanted to insulate their currencies from economic realities, they established exchange controls, meaning that they allowed only small amounts of their domestic currency out, or of other currencies in. They also prohibited domestic monetary gold markets. The dictators and their followers required foreign trade partners to deal with them through so-called "clearing" accounts. A German buyer of, say, Swiss products would make his deal. He would then deposit the price, in reichsmarks, in a special "clearing" account in Berlin, the managers of which notified the Swiss authorities that the price had been paid. The Swiss authorities would then guarantee that an equivalent amount of domestic currency had been placed in a clearing account in Switzerland, from which the seller could draw his payment. Any Swiss who bought products in Germany would deposit the price in Swiss francs into the Swiss clearing account, and then be authorized to draw on the reichsmarks in the German clearing account to pay his seller. Thus, clearing accounts in each country would be replenished by buyers and sellers. Although the system was supposed to keep international trade in balance, one country's buyers sometimes ran up bills amounting to more than its sellers' deposits. Then the second country's government would make short-term deposits into the clearing account, effectively granting a line of credit both to domestic sellers and to foreign buyers. Some countries ran up clearing deficits that they would not clear promptly, effectively establishing long-term lines of credit for themselves and their suppliers. Because the value of the currencies of the countries that practiced exchange controls depended on negotiations with each of their trading partners, the system introduced an element of force into peacetime trade.

Now consider the demands that the Reich's negotiators presented to the Swiss as German armies were surrounding their country in 1940. First, the Germans ordered the Swiss to forget about their War Trade Agreement with Britain, since Swiss industries were about to receive a set of orders from the Reich to be filled urgently. These orders, not any agreements, would set the limits to the quantities of arms Switzerland would deliver to the Reich. Even the arms the Allies had contracted for were to be delivered to the Reich. Second, the Germans stated that, since the value of their orders would be much greater than that of any goods the Reich was planning to send to Switzerland, there would be a clearing deficit of at least 150 million francs—which the Swiss would finance. All in all, a bad deal.

When the Swiss balked, the Germans shut off the coal.

The Swiss tried to yield in a way that preserved the semblance of normal trade. In exchange for coal at the Reich's price, Germany would get its war goods, and on credit. But

Switzerland had to continue honoring at least some part of the agreement with Britain. Indeed, from the German perspective, without the *navicerts* that went along with Swiss production for Britain, the Reich would have to help feed Switzerland, and Swiss industry could not produce all sorts of things the Reich wanted.

No sooner was the ink dry, however, than it became clear that the clearing deficit would be bigger than had been agreed upon—the Germans were taking more and giving less. By July 1941 Reich orders and nonpayments forced yet another round of negotiations, which more than doubled the credit line— which had already more than doubled in an agreement from the previous summer—this time to 815 million francs. After this, the farce of negotiations was abandoned, and the credit line rose uncontrolled to something like 1.25 billion francs until 1943. Credit (sure to be unredeemed) ended up accounting for more than half of the merchandise exports to Germany.

That, however, did not mean that the Reich really paid for the remaining half of its imports from Switzerland, because the Reich delivered less and less of the coal, oil, and other essential materials that were part of the deal, and charged higher prices for them. In 1939 Switzerland had paid 129 million francs for about three million tons of coal from a variety of sources. In 1942 it paid a total of 168 million francs for a little less than two million tons, 96 percent of it from the Reich.[3] In other words, the effective price of coal went up from 43 francs per ton to 88 per ton. The barbarian's sword weighed heavy on the balance.

Consider the practical side of this arrangement. While the "clearing credits" piled up abstractly in Berlin, Swiss workers and suppliers, both foreign and domestic, had to be paid with real francs. Where did these francs come from? The Swiss National Bank printed them. But since few consumer goods were coming in or being produced, Swiss workers faced potentially disastrous inflation. The Swiss National Bank, however, sold the debt to the government, which issued bonds to sop up the cash. In short, to avoid inflation, the Swiss people were induced to buy what were, indirectly, the Reich's war bonds.

Why did the Swiss political system agree to this? In part because the captains of heavy industry, the *Vorort*, and their workers were pushing for it. These Swiss citizens were delivering real merchandise to the Reich and getting paid with real Swiss money, even though all this produced net losses for Swiss society as a whole. The point was, Swiss workers and industrialists hated the Reich less than they loved their paychecks. It is a familiar reality of modern interest-group politics: A part of society manages to get the whole to subsidize a set of jobs and investments. It does not matter if the products are wasted or even if they go to enemies of the whole. During the Cold War, for example, a mighty lobby arose in the United States for shipping all sorts of goods to the Soviet Union. The industries involved were paid in good dollars corresponding to bad loans guaranteed by the U.S. government. And in the 1990s many American businesses were selling to China with loan guarantees from the taxpayer-financed U.S. Export-Import Bank, or were operating in China or Vietnam with capital guaranteed by the U.S. Overseas Private Investment Corporation. In other words, the American public was buying Soviet, and later Chinese, war bonds.

What did the Reich get out of the arrangement with Swiss industry? Out of the total 2.5 billion francs in merchandise, about 1.35 billion was strategic materials. Of this some 600 million (28 percent of the total) was arms and ammunition, while the rest was machine tools (the biggest category), fuses and other timing devices, precision tools, and aluminum. The Germans also got about a billion francs' worth of excellent dairy products. Moreover, the Reich took an average of a billion kilowatt-hours per year of electricity from the Swiss hydroelectric grid—12 percent of domestic production.[4] In sum, during the war years Nazi Germany took an average of over twice as much from Switzerland as it had in 1938—but concentrated on war goods.

What benefits did Switzerland receive? As it produced arms for the Reich, it kept some to build up its own army. The coal, oil, and other imports allowed by Germany were just enough to keep the Swiss economy together. The Third Reich milked Switzerland almost as if it had been occupied—but not quite. The clearing deficit for Germany ended up at about 7 percent of Swiss GDP (as much as 12 percent if one factors in higher prices for German goods), whereas countries that either had been occupied or were allied, such as Romania, wound up despoiled at three to four times that ratio. So, Switzerland's trade with the Reich was about cutting losses, not getting rich.

On July 18, 1941, as the Soviet armies were surrendering by the millions, Reich negotiators forced the Federal Council to prohibit Swiss citizens from sending parcels abroad. The Germans had learned these parcels were used to fill British orders for the jewel bearings. Now they felt strong enough to stop it.

When the parcels stopped arriving in Britain, the British retaliated by eliminating *navicerts* for Switzerland except for food, tobacco, and "compensating exports," which allowed goods to be imported to manufacture exports that the Germans would permit.

The jewel-bearing traffic now traveled by human smugglers, organized by Swiss manufacturers and the British Embassy. As late as July 1944, while the U.S. Army was driving up the Rhône valley, American soldiers captured two suspicious men who, it turned out, were part of this traffic.[5] The Germans, who were generally more interested in exploiting the continent than in preventing its resources from leaking out, allowed the Swiss to sell watches for food. But the Swiss often used these sales to slip fine chronometer movements past the Germans by omitting the watch's third hand. So, even in the dark days of 1942, as Switzerland was delivering 656 million francs in merchandise on credit to Germany, it managed to export 310 million francs' worth of merchandise to the Allies.

Discussions between the Swiss and the Allies in 1942 consisted of polite Allied requests that the Swiss reduce their favors to the enemy, and Swiss protestations that they would like nothing better but could not do it. By the spring of 1943, however, the changing relative weight of swords meant that the Allies could squeeze the Swiss harder and that the Swiss could transfer some of their new pain to the Germans with less fear of dire consequences. In April 1943 the Allies cut off all food to Switzerland, a big sanction, and demanded something rather small—a reduction of 20 percent in industrial deliveries to Germany over the second half of 1943 as compared to the previous year, plus a cessation of credits to the Reich. In return, they promised to restore *half* the food shipments. In June the Swiss agreed.

The Germans had told the Swiss to reject the Allied terms, but by 1943 they were unable to punish Swiss disobedience. If the Reich cut off coal, the Swiss would stop all industrial deliveries. If Germany invaded—which made less sense for the

Wehrmacht after its losses at Stalingrad and Kursk—Swiss industrial production would have to be restarted and reorganized. A Reich Ministry of Armaments memo of June 3, 1943, stated that although Swiss deliveries amounted to only 0.5 percent of Reich procurement, they were too important to be disrupted. Better to suffer shrinkage than disruption.[6] Hence, the most efficient course of action for Germany was to take what exports the balance of power would give and to start paying cash for them. It was a sober calculation, despite the sensational claims of historian Werner Rings, who wrote that deliveries from unbombed Switzerland were big enough to make up for Allied bomb damage to German industry.[7] In reality, Swiss production was both too small to fight over and too big to disrupt. Again, we see that the terms of wartime trade can be set only by the balance of power.

No sooner had the June 1943 agreement taken hold than the changing balance of power allowed the Allies to cast it aside and demand tighter restrictions. Since the Allies could not impose greater pain on the Swiss in the present, they gave a concrete example of the huge pain they could dish out in the future. The Anglo-American negotiators had gotten to know a Swiss delegate, Dr. Hans Sulzer, the head of a powerful company who was known for supporting the Allies. The Allies placed his firm on the blacklist, banning it from any world trade after the prospective Allied victory. It was a warning to the captains of Swiss industry. If the Allies could ruin Sulzer, they could ruin anybody. Unless Swiss industrialists accepted the pain of detaching from the German war economy, they would be ruined after the war. Sulzer's name stayed on the list only a month. On December 19, 1943, to get Sulzer off the list and forestall further blacklisting, the Swiss government agreed to slash trade with the Reich by 50 percent in highly specific categories. In high-tech fields, reductions averaged 60 percent. In cheese, the Swiss cut 100 percent of trade.[8] The Germans were furious, but now it was less worthwhile to invade Switzerland than it had been months earlier. By this time, the Germans would get what they could.

Until the third quarter of 1944 the Allies still had no power to offer Switzerland military protection, and no capacity to fulfill any of its economic needs. But by 1943 they had already gained power over the future. The German trade negotiators must have marveled at how the Allies were fine-tuning Swiss trade from far away. In 1944 the Allies pressed new demands, and by August of that year the Swiss had agreed to cut the previously agreed-on quotas in half again.

The final stroke against German economic domination of Switzerland came on one of the first trains to Geneva through liberated France. The train carried no economic goods to tip the balance, but rather an Allied delegation headed by Lauchlin Currie, assistant to the president of the United States. Along with his British counterpart, Dingle Foot, Currie told the Swiss that the Allies wanted Germany to receive no militarily useful items. Above all, they wanted Switzerland to stop Germany's railroad traffic through the Alpine tunnels. Complying with the first demand was legally easy; the Federal Council banned all shipments of arms and ammunition, to *any* country. The second was tougher, for the Reich had an undeniable legal right to use the tunnels. But the Swiss could no more afford to alienate the new masters of the continent by continuing to comply with the 1909 tunnel treaty than they had been able to afford, in 1940, to alienate the masters of *that* hour by complying with the War Trade Agreement of April 25, 1940. So the Swiss stopped the traffic, violating their obligation to Germany as they had earlier violated their deal with Britain.

This, emphatically, is not to say that Swiss politicians treated the two sets of obligations as morally or politically equivalent. On the contrary, the Currie delegation was greeted with spontaneous joy wherever it went, because it represented the lifting of a horrible incubus. Rather, the point is that the vast qualitative differences between the Nazis and the Allies could not efface the fact that their military capacities were commensurable.

Even as Allied victory loomed, Switzerland faced tighter economic restrictions. After all, through 1944 Switzerland got 97 percent of its coal from Germany, and almost that much in 1945. As the deliveries from Germany were stopping, no one could foresee when or from where the next trainload of coal, other fuels, or metals was coming. Nevertheless, the Swiss recognized that the day's principal business was to determine the kind of life that the world would live after the war, and thus they were delighted that their economic problems were being imposed by a future Allied victory rather than by continuing German extortion.

Money and Gold

The war forced the world to conduct ordinary economic dealings in hard currency—that is, in currency universally acceptable and reconvertible to gold. But World War II also shrank the supply of such currencies and cut the number of monetary gold markets. Until 1939 the world's hard currencies were the U.S. dollar, the British pound sterling, and the Swiss franc. In that year, however, the pound sterling lost its status as a hard currency when Britain declared war. Instead of using the London money markets, Germany bought dollars in New

York with Swiss francs. In July 1941 the dollar, too, ceased to be a hard currency, when the government froze European assets in the United States. When America entered the war, the U.S. Treasury would still exchange foreign banks' dollars for gold, but the gold would be frozen in American vaults. The only currency that could still be exchanged for gold (and the gold carried away) was the Swiss franc.

Demand for the Swiss franc was widespread, as was the demand for gold, among the Axis, the Allies, the neutrals, and the occupied peoples. After the Allies froze the two-thirds of Swiss gold reserves that had been sent to New York and London for safekeeping—stripping the franc of its normal backing—the Swiss National Bank had a strong incentive to buy gold with francs, in a very competitive market, to support the franc. Unfortunately, because imports and consumer-good production levels were very low, printing so many francs created a "currency overhang" that portended inflation. Hence the bank was being forced to fight against the insolvency of its currency at the risk of inflating it. Moreover, as the Reich and the Allies exchanged gold for francs and foreign currencies under their own special conditions, and as Portuguese, Spaniards, and Romanians reconverted francs and other currencies for gold, and as countless private parties bought up gold, the Swiss economy was mightily troubled.

Riding this tiger was an inescapable consequence of Switzerland's remaining a free, open economy. Had the Swiss government tried to eliminate the gold-currency imbalances by shutting down the gold market and outlawing the circulation of foreign currencies—that is, if it had tried to introduce exchange controls and bilateral clearing accounts with each trading partner—it would have impossibly complicated commercial relations already shrunken and deformed by the war. Even in normal times Switzerland's trade with the rest of the world was highly unbalanced, and under the constraints of blockade and counterblockade Switzerland's gold-backed currency had become perhaps its most valuable resource. If Switzerland refused to let the Allies convert their gold into francs, the United States and Britain might retaliate by cutting *navicerts*. If the Swiss refused Germany's gold trade, they would eliminate one of the main reasons why the Reich respected Swiss independence.

Already by the end of 1940 the Reichsbank had noted the usefulness of Switzerland's free financial market. In November of that year Per Jacobson, counselor of the Basel-based Bank of International Settlements, reported to Swiss National Bank Chairman Eugen Weber on a conversation with Emil Pohl, vice president of the Reichsbank:

> [Talking of Swedish exchange controls] I said to him that it was important for Europe that the Swiss currency remain free, so that there would exist on this continent a strong currency with which to negotiate after the war. Mr. Pohl agreed, and added that Switzerland's abstinence from exchange controls was also important from the political standpoint because it is a reason for leaving Switzerland free.[9]

Weber passed this on to the Federal Council. But at that point Swiss currency, though important, was not vital to Germany because the Reich believed it had already won the war. Not until a year later, when the Russian campaign stalled, did Germany think seriously about total economic mobilization.

Only then did the Reichsbank start taking full advantage of the Swiss money market.

Keep in mind that what followed—the conversion of some 1.2 billion francs' worth of gold from the Reichsbank to the Swiss National Bank into francs and other currencies—was not, as Werner Rings charges, "the transformation of Nazi gold into Swiss gold."[10] Most of that gold—781 million francs' worth—stayed "Swiss" only long enough for the Reich's central bank customers, to whom Germany had paid francs for merchandise, to convert their francs into Spanish or Portuguese or Romanian gold. Only a small part of the francs bought by the Reich was spent in Switzerland (after 1943 in real payment for merchandise) and thus did not undergo reconversion. By contrast, most of the francs purchased by the Allies were not reconverted (see below). In a nutshell, the Reich used the Swiss money market primarily to launder its gold. And nobody was innocent about how much laundering that gold needed.

So, Rings's principal contention, that Nazi gold mightily enriched the Swiss, is untrue. The Swiss National Bank kept only 28 million francs in brokerage fees—just 2.5 percent of the total. The commercial banks also were in the gold business primarily as brokers. Their balance sheets for the war years show that the gold trade added between 1 percent and 3 percent to their profits.[11]

Rings and the other conspiracy theorists say that the gold trade was the idea of Paul Rossy, vice president of the Swiss National Bank, to enrich Switzerland and that the Swiss got the Germans to go along.[12] But the Swiss gained little from the transaction, and the Nazis certainly had no incentive to enrich another country. No, the gold trade was not anybody's idea. As we've seen, it was inherent in a situation where the Reich had gold and needed raw materials, the suppliers were subject to Allied pressure and demanded payment in clean, hard currency, the Swiss franc was the only gold-convertible currency, and Switzerland was the only country with a free market for monetary exchange. Most implausible of all is the notion that the Reich went along with a scheme to enrich anyone. The Reich was not an eleemosynary institution.

The situation was hardly comfortable for Swiss currency managers. All sorts of people saw gold as the safest wartime investment and were buying large quantities of gold coins. Prominent among them were European holders of credit balances in Switzerland, who converted their balances to gold, raising the metal's price. This in turn led to financial speculation by Swiss banks.[13] For example, a commercial bank might purchase a Swiss "Vreneli" coin from the National Bank at the official price of 30 francs and sell it to the public for 40, which added to inflationary pressure. To keep gold's price below 215 grains per franc, the National Bank was obliged to sell gold into the market, thus depleting its reserves and creating more francs. By mid-1940 the National Bank's gold stock had fallen below the 40 percent of the outstanding franc value that it was statutorily required to keep. A secret ordinance repealed the statute. By mid-1941 the amount in the vault dropped to 600 million francs, 31 percent of the value of francs on the street. The combination of German and private maneuvers on the gold market was draining gold from the treasury and undermining the franc.

That is why in mid-1941 the National Bank asked the Reichsbank informally to channel its gold transactions in Switzerland through official channels at Switzerland's fixed price. On December 9, 1942, the Swiss government put in place the other half of its plan: It limited gold trading to licensees, banned sales of Swiss gold coins, and tried to impose an official price for private transactions in gold. Again, the point was not to get rich, *but to cut losses*. The channeling arrangement and the attempt at market regulations did not much affect the burgeoning black market. Some Swiss banks opened gold accounts in Turkey or Argentina and traded telegraphically. The black market price kept rising. But the agreement did ensure that foreign central banks would take out of the National Bank no more gold than the Reichsbank put in. The government's formal withdrawal from the domestic market stabilized the price of monetary gold. All this stopped the hemorrhage from the bank's reserves and took speculative pressure off the franc.

The Swiss government and National Bank had always seen the gold trade with Germany as a perilous political necessity rather than as a means of making money. In addition to the 28 million francs in brokerage fees, the bank made another 20 million in the coin trade, which amounted to a little more than half of its wartime profits—but these profits were not large. Indeed, the bank existed to protect the integrity of the currency rather than to profit. Paul Rossy was the only director who really liked the gold trade, and that, not for economic reasons, but because he thought it would earn his country a place in the "New Europe." That idea had faded by 1943. The rest of the bank's board and the government treated the German gold trade with the proverbial ten-foot pole.

The first gold shipment from the Reichsbank arrived at the Swiss National Bank in March 1940, unannounced. The Swiss bank's policy had been to welcome gold sales only as part of commercial transactions. It considered sending the gold back. But, to avoid an embarrassing confrontation, it credited to the Reichsbank the gold's value of 9 million francs. In February, after a Swiss commercial bank had accepted a shipment of Soviet gold from Berlin, the National Bank let it be known that "such gold transactions are not favored."[14] In May, twice as much German gold as the initial German load was dropped on the bank's doorstep. This time the bank advised the Germans that such sales were not welcome, but said that it would make an exception for Germany and buy its gold outside of a commercial context. Some Swiss naively hoped that the Reich could be induced to start paying for its imports with gold. Still, in early 1940, the Swiss believed that they were not starting down a slippery slope because the U.S. dollar, not the franc, was going to be the international currency. If anything, they expected the Germans to use Switzerland to buy dollars. By June, however, after the fall of France, the bank's board and the government had begun looking at German gold conversions as a price to pay for the Reich's goodwill.[15] But the National Bank's negative attitude is also the reason why the Reichsbank initially converted its gold primarily at commercial banks.

Convenience ruled the Reichsbank's gold operations. It did not always buy francs; sometimes, it bought escudos or pesetas or krona directly. It also shipped to the Swiss National Bank some 400 million francs' worth of gold that it did not convert at all, but transferred either directly to the lockers that other central banks kept in Bern or to its own locker there. In 1940–1941 it even shipped to Bern 60 million francs' worth of gold from the Soviet Union that the Swiss were to redeem for dollars in New York and then remit to Berlin, presumably for Moscow.

The Reich did not particularly like to sell gold, but as it had to use more and more real money abroad it sold with abandon and with a keen eye for maximizing returns. After selling 141 million francs' worth in 1941, Germany jumped to

424 million francs' worth the following year. In 1943 it sold only 370 million, but a third of that amount was made up of coins sold at a premium, and after 1943 some of the Reich's gold sales to Switzerland actually paid for Swiss products.

Swiss authorities were uncomfortable with the traffic from the beginning for three reasons: the profits it generated were not worth the financial turmoil it caused; the traffic made the Allies unhappy because it was so valuable to Germany; and, of course, at least some of the gold was dirty.

We have already seen how slim a percentage of the German gold traffic returned directly to the banks. But what about the bottom line for the country? In 1939 Swiss gold reserves totaled 2.8 billion francs. At the end of the war they totaled 4.6 billion. But the latter figure includes *net* purchases from the Allies of 2.2 billion francs' worth of gold. To see the net effect on Swiss gold reserves of the German gold traffic, just subtract the Allies' sales from the postwar bottom line. With German traffic alone, the Swiss would have wound up with about one-seventh *less* gold than before the war. The only net gain came from the National Bank's purchase of gold from the Allies, which was frozen in New York. The postwar gnomes of Zurich's gold was American, not Nazi.

As early as 1940 Swiss authorities noted the American Embassy's displeasure with Germany's use of Swiss financial markets. By 1943 the United States and Britain were warning the neutrals that they would not recognize their ownership of gold that the Nazis had stolen from Europe. This was always more of a moral statement than a realistic threat, because stolen gold was *spent* and could not be recovered without somehow despoiling a new set of innocents in a chain stretching from Portuguese tungsten miners to their suppliers and middlemen.

To what extent could the Allies punish the Swiss for having been part of the traffic? Once the money was spent, it was gone. By 1944 the Allies had shelved moral admonitions and, as belligerents, demanded that the Portuguese and Spanish stop selling merchandise to the Germans and that the Swiss stop converting Axis gold—or risk being treated like enemies.

The moral side of the equation was never in doubt. The Hague Convention of 1907 prohibited occupying powers from taking the property, and especially the gold, of private parties. That the Nazis were thieves as well as murderers was not news. Nor was it news that a special Nazi police unit had been formed to enforce (often with the death penalty) decrees in Germany itself as well as in occupied countries, obliging individuals to exchange personal gold possessions, including wedding rings, for paper currency. The Nazis called this program to steal private gold the "Four-Year Plan." Eventually, according to a U.S. government postwar audit of the Reichsbank, the program yielded $71.8 million worth of gold.[16] The most infamous kind of gold theft, the extraction of prisoners' last possessions at labor-death camps, surely yielded at least the $2.9 million worth that was deposited in the Reichsbank in the so-called Melmer account. Although the amount of "victim gold" was much greater than that, it is essential to note that the Reich apparently never smelted the bulk of victim gold, some $30 million worth of it, and that therefore this gold never entered international circulation. American forces in Thuringia in 1945 found boxes and boxes of wedding rings and dental gold; apparently, the recipients in the Reichsbank had not dared turn it over to ordinary employees of the mint, lest they be scandalized. After all, the Holocaust was a state secret, and boxes of wedding rings and dental fillings would have repelled even most Nazis. Americans discovered and took possession of the Reichsbank's cache (and made films of these ghastly prizes). American, not Swiss, authorities smelted this victim gold, and did so *after* the war. Nevertheless, the possibility—indeed, the likelihood—that some indeterminable amount of the gold in the Swiss-German traffic came from blatantly illegal sources was always clear and present.

The Reich also appropriated large amounts of gold in circumstances that were not so clearly illegal. The government of the Netherlands actually lent its entire gold reserves to the Reich, and the pro-Nazi head of its national bank signed a piece of paper to the effect that it was doing so of its own will. Of course, since the Nazis had just occupied the country, a reasonable person might conclude that the Dutch government's will was about as free as that of the Romans who were paying off Brennus. The Reich also got the two-thirds of the Belgian gold reserves that Brussels had sent to the Banque de France; the Vichy government handed them over. Since Vichy had no legal right to do so, the Reich had no right to Belgian gold—except for one fact. The Hague Convention does allow belligerents to take possession of enemy *governments'* possessions, including gold. If central banks are considered "independent" of governments, the Reich's possession of gold from Dutch, Belgian, Hungarian, Italian, and other central banks was illegal spoliation of private property. If central banks are government organs, then under international law their spoils belong to the victor.

The Reichsbank, however, always claimed that the gold it was selling abroad came entirely from its own prewar stocks. That claim is not as ridiculous as might appear from mid-1939 German statements of reserves, including Austrian and Czech stocks—a mere $256 million worth (or close to 1 billion Swiss francs' worth). In fact, the Swiss National Bank estimated pre-1940 Reich stocks at 1.5 billion francs. And during the twenty-one months of the Stalin–Hitler Pact, the Soviet Union shipped to Germany very large (and as yet unknown) amounts of gold to purchase German weapons and to finance its own purchases in the rest of the world. This may have almost doubled German stocks.[17]

At any rate, through 1942 the Reichsbank had shipped to the Swiss National Bank only 700 million francs' worth of gold—arguably within German pre-1940 reserves, every ingot bearing the seal of the Reichsbank.

The intra-Swiss debate about the legality of the Reich's gold began in 1943, when the Germans traded for francs larger amounts of Belgian "Lator" gold coins than the Reichsbank was known to have, and when German gold shipments were reaching dubiously high levels. The Allies said none of the gold was legitimate. The Germans said all of it was. But apart from the Belgian coins, the Swiss had no hard evidence that the gold was not German. On that basis, the bank limited its acceptance of gold to ingots, and asked the Germans no longer to convert gold for the purpose of buying third-country currencies. In other words, it preferred to take gold only in payment for Swiss merchandise.

But two practical problems prevented the National Bank and the Federal Council from cutting off the German gold trade. First, as mentioned, by 1943 the trade had ceased to harm the Swiss economy. It was finally bolstering the franc and bringing in real payments. Stopping it would wreck the franc and perhaps result in economic siege by the Reich. Second, the only practically conceivable way of stopping the German gold trade—the only way that stood even a dim chance of avoiding the most violent German reactions—was to close down the Swiss gold market to all foreigners at once. But by 1943 the gold trade with the Allies had become much bigger than that with the Germans. Stopping it would wreck the economy from the other end, and anger the Allies.

Thus, the bank and the council took the middle route. But their tactic of justifying their actions by pointing to international law rather than the economic and military balance of power won them no friends.

Allied Trade

Even in the war's darkest years, 1941 and 1942, exports to the Allies, mostly to the United States and the "dollar zone" of Latin America, never fell below 17 percent of total Swiss exports. By 1943 they were over 20 percent. Swiss industry never earned less than 300 million francs in Allied countries, and usually made more. Unlike exports to Germany, however, these were paid in real money, converted to gold, but "frozen" in Allied vaults. By contrast with the gold bought from the Reich, which stayed "Swiss" only until it was reconverted to Portuguese, Spanish, Swedish, or Turkish ownership, most of the gold sold by the Allies would remain Swiss. To this were added the dollars (converted to gold) earned by Swiss investments, mostly in the United States but also in Britain. Also, since Switzerland was among the top five foreign investors in America ($1.4 billion, prewar), the returns were considerable, up to $100 million per year. And since the blockade prevented the Swiss from spending all but a pittance of this money for imports, Swiss gold piled up in New York. To keep Swiss exporters in business, the National Bank advanced them the franc equivalent of their New York balances in exchange for title to the frozen gold. The bank sold the debt to the government. The government in turn "sterilized" the debt by selling bonds. So the Swiss people were indirectly buying American war bonds, too. By the end of the war the bank, the government, and major investors had title to about $1.5 billion either in gold or holdings convertible to gold—almost $400 for every man, woman, and child in Switzerland. In addition, the $1.4 billion of Swiss investments in the United States had grown substantially in value.

Yet this ultimately lucrative arrangement posed immediate difficulties. In 1943 Swiss watch exports to the West rose dramatically while at the same time the Allies, mostly the United States, started buying massive amounts of Swiss francs for their various operations in Europe (as well as for relief of Allied prisoners). How was the Swiss economy going to finance all of this? At first, fearing inflation, the Swiss National Bank and the government refused to buy up the watch exporters' entire credit balances. At the same time the Allied gold sales were creating massive amounts of francs unsupported by gold in Bern.

Mitigating these problems from the demand side proved impossible. The watchmakers, led by able lobbyist Max Petitpierre, launched a powerful campaign for full funding. The Allies supported the watchmakers' claims on the Swiss government, saying that Switzerland's failure to support the watchmakers would be taken as a sign of pro-German partiality. So, long-term hope and fear of the Allies overcame short-term fear of inflation and the Germans. The authorities stepped in and bought the full commercial debt.

But how could the Swiss put real, disposable gold under the franc to prevent immediate, rampant inflation? The answer was the Reichsbank, which was an eager supplier of gold, some of which, after 1943, had good prospects of remaining "Swiss." Buying gold from Germany made it possible for Switzerland to buy gold from the Allies—good for the long term, without going broke in the near term. In part, Germany's economic warfare measures, using (tainted) gold, enabled the Allies to carry out their financial warfare measures with clean Swiss francs. Given the balance of power and geography, the Allies could not have had the benefits of Swiss watches and jewel bearings, or Swiss francs for that matter, if the Reich had not benefited from Swiss machine tools, electricity, and of course Swiss francs.

The balancing act ended in March 1945, when Switzerland banned all trading of foreign currencies. But by then the Allies needed no more help, and the Germans were beyond doing harm.

Safe Haven?

In Judeo-Christian civilization, property rights derive from work because man, by working, joins God's creative function. John Locke secularized this tradition by arguing that things belong to those who mix their labor with them. Thus while all mankind might theoretically own the coal under the earth, the coal actually belongs to the workers and capitalists who dig it up. But in war, things belong to those with the power to take them. The same is true in interest-group politics.

Before the twentieth century, widely held Christian just-war precepts gave noncombatants reasonable hope for the safety of their property. As late as 1907 (by which time the Boer War had already portended its futility) the Hague Convention specified that armies must not appropriate the goods of enemy civilians. But in the very first war of the enlightened twentieth century,

Germany despoiled and enslaved the Belgians and Frenchmen whose land it occupied. After World War I the century's worst regimes—the Third Reich and the Soviet Union—were founded on a permanent declaration of war against the Jews and the "class enemy," respectively. Even before the Second World War these regimes despoiled their enemies not for anything they did but for who they were. During that war they inflicted spoliation, enslavement, and worse on all the peoples they conquered. Consequently, Europe was full of innocents scurrying to save their lives and property. By the end of the war even the best regimes, Britain's and America's, had adopted the practices of the worst. They bombed civilians. When they won, they claimed title to all the property in Germany (including cutting down German forests to sell the lumber) and conscripted civilians for labor in exchange for bare survival rations. They also claimed the property of any German anywhere in the world.

Switzerland's experience in World War II shows how problematic it is, especially for a small country, to be an economic safe haven in wartime. Nazi victims and innocent Germans (yes, there were such beings) tried, along with Nazis, to shelter their assets under Swiss laws. At the end of the war, however, the Swiss government joined the Allies not just in appropriating the assets of the Nazi regime but also in imposing a penalty on the assets of ordinary Germans. No one disputed that the assets of victims ought to be returned to them or to their heirs. Nor has there ever been an argument that assets without heirs should somehow be devoted to the common good. But the modalities of restitution have had much less to do with property rights than with rapacious interest-group politics.

Allied economic warriors remembered that after World War I German companies had spun off weapons-building subsidiaries to other countries. Zeiss built its military optics in the Netherlands. Junkers machinery went to Sweden and Russia. Krupp exchanged stock with Bofors of Sweden for the privilege of building heavy guns there. As World War II wound down, the Allies thought they noticed extensive plans for a Nazi revival. According to Allied economic warriors: "There were widespread rumors of [the Nazis'] purchasing properties in the neutral countries—industrial establishments, real estate, financial companies—and buying into neutral business concerns, often under disguise or through an agent. Sizable bank accounts were reported open in safe places.... The Nazis were preparing to go underground, they were seeking a safe haven...."[18] Consequently, Bretton Woods Resolution VI endorsed Allied policy to "uncover, control, and dispose of enemy assets" as well as to undo some of the Nazis' most egregious thefts of private property, especially artworks.

Thus, Allied economic warriors inventoried German assets around the world. In the Allied countries German assets had already been seized regardless of whether they were the property of the government, corporations, or individuals. In Germany itself the Soviets were dismantling and carrying off everything they could, including thousands upon thousands of German slave laborers. At the Potsdam Conference the Allies laid permanent claim to all German assets outside Germany. This meant that in the United States, Britain, and France, all property of any kind belonging to any and all citizens of Germany was "vested" in the government. The original U.S. executive order (9567, June 1945) "vesting" all "enemy property" made no distinction between guilty, innocent, and victim. The U.S. government turned over about half of the $900 million in proceeds to the Allies' German External Property Commission and kept the other half to pay American claims, such as those of former prisoners of war. In their negotiations with neutral governments, the Allies asked them to "vest" in the commission all Germans' property within their borders.

By mid-1945 fear of a Nazi revival had faded. Nevertheless the victors' hunger for "enemy property" did not diminish.

The practical justification was obvious. Because of Germany, all had suffered and spent much more than they could possibly recover. Hence, they should recover as much as they could. Germany's war had not discriminated between private and public assets. All Germans had somehow contributed to the war effort, and all were somehow responsible. The moral and legal justification was more difficult. The very existence of Nazi victims showed the absurdity of treating every German as an enemy to be despoiled. Was there, moreover, to be no more distinction between public and private? And what about the neutrals? Had they no legitimate claims against Germany?

Since most German property abroad was corporate, little objective argument could be made about its innocence or guilt. Allies and neutrals presumed it guilty and seized it. But the same reasons that led Allied governments to take it for themselves— they had lots of claims against Germany and these assets would barely scratch the surface—also moved the neutrals to help themselves to the assets of German foreign subsidiaries. As for the Swiss, U.S. economic warriors David L. Gordon and Royden Dangerfield quipped that "by coincidence" they had estimated the value of German assets in their country at just about the 1.2 billion francs that the Reich owed Switzerland to clear the 1940–1943 Swiss advances in the clearing account. Then, Gordon and Dangerfield reported, when the Allies argued that German assets in Switzerland were worth three times as much as the Swiss had estimated, "the Swiss brought up other claims against Germany to make up a comparable amount." In the end the matter was settled with less nobility than practicality: The two sides established a joint commission to set the value, and the Swiss contributed to the Allied fund precisely what the United States had, namely 50 percent of German corporate property, and kept the other half.

By the same token, the 1946 American-Swiss bargain over Swiss handling of looted gold from Germany was about money rather than principle. U.S. negotiators did not try to argue that Swiss trade with Germany or conversion of gold from the Reich was wrong under international law. They could hardly do that since they had traded with the enemy in small ways and of course exchanged gold for Swiss francs. But they said that the Swiss would have to redeem themselves for having gotten too close to the enemy, and because an indeterminable percentage of the gold they bought from the Reich was dirty. The Americans' best argument, however, was the more than $3 billion of Swiss assets still frozen in the United States. The Swiss for their part cited both international law and necessity, but they knew they were going to have to pay something to get back their frozen assets. The negotiations were about how big a ransom to pay; there is no other objective validity to the final figure of $58 million (or 250 million francs) that the Swiss government paid to the Allies as part of the 1946 agreement which normalized Switzerland's economic relations with the Allies.

For small German accounts—those worth less than 10,000 francs—the Swiss government tried to maintain the principle of the inviolability of private property, but in the end, under American pressure, the Swiss compromised and froze the accounts. In 1949, working with the new government of the Federal Republic of Germany, Switzerland unfroze the small accounts but took for itself one-third of the assets therein. It too exacted a ransom commensurate with its power.

In essence, postwar financial settlements followed two principles: possession is anywhere between 50 and 100 percent of the law, and the strong keep what they can while the weak give up what they must.

The United States at first applied these laws strictly. Jewish organizations waged a long, bitter, and small-fruited campaign to get the U.S. government to introduce proper nuance in its treatment of "enemy property." The easy part of the campaign ended in Public Law 6761 of August 1946, which directed the American custodian of enemy property to restore property seized from Germans (mostly Jews) who could prove that they had been victims of Nazi persecution. To get their property back, applicants (prominent enough and lucky enough to have established title to property in the United States) had to show that they had actually suffered persecution. Of course they also had to be alive, or their heirs had to have lots of proof. Because of rumors that some Jews who had perished in the Holocaust (and who had relatives in the United States) had bank accounts in New York, Jewish organizations urged the U.S. government to prevail on New York State to make and publish a list of such accounts. Had the state done this, claimants of the accounts would have faced formidable hurdles. The first would have been to prove that the account holder was indeed dead. But that would not have been enough, since state law prohibited giving private property to relatives without a will. But the state government refused to make an inventory until 1954. So the Jewish organizations and the government lobbied the New York legislature to turn the balance over to (who else) these organizations themselves—to no avail. In the end, whatever money might have been in such heirless accounts ended up "escheating" to New York State.

Since this outcome was already clear in 1949, the Jewish organizations began lobbying Congress and the administration to turn over to them an amount presumed equivalent to any "heirless assets." Senate Bill 603, supported by the Truman administration, proposed to do that, and to "set an upper limit of $3 million."[19] The committee report on the Senate bill stated the conclusion of "experts" who estimated the value of such accounts in the United States at between $500,000 and $2 million. The report did not specify the data on which the "experts" based this huge spread. How could anyone have defended any estimate, short of conducting an investigation into the personal history of every holder of a dormant bank account? So S-603 died. In subsequent rhetorical campaigns, the Jewish groups seeking U.S. government compensation never offered evidence for the amount of money they were seeking, nor did they explain why they rather than some other persons should get to handle the money. In the 1950s, since the World Jewish Congress's pull with the Eisenhower administration was nil, it got nothing. It was somewhat greater with the Kennedy administration, which decided to distribute $500,000 to Jewish organizations to end the matter.

But it didn't end there. The 1949 report on S-603 contained the following sentence: "It is generally recognized that depositories for the assets of deceased minority victims are in Switzerland and the United States." The report could not offer evidence about the size of such assets in Switzerland any more than it could about assets in the United States. Nonetheless, such guesswork has created the widespread impression that Switzerland absorbed massive amounts of Jewish flight capital, that most of the depositors perished, and that the leftovers were enough to constitute Switzerland's wealth—and its shame. Prior to 1995 the impression came from two myths.

The first, purveyed by generations of Swiss bankers and credulous journalists, has it that in 1934 the Swiss government wrote a new banking law—including the famous Clause 47(b) that penalizes any Swiss who reveals information about any Swiss bank account—in order to protect the Swiss banks' numerous German Jewish customers who were threatened by the Nazi death penalty for taking money abroad. The full florid version of this innocent myth is found in *L'Argent Secret et les Banques Suisses* by Jean Marie Laya, former economics news editor of the *Journal de Genève*. It tells of Nazi spies ferreting out Jewish account holders in Swiss banks, of clever bank counterspies, and of the clause as the ultimate weapon against the Nazis.

All nonsense. The first draft of the new banking law was published in February 1933, just a few weeks after Hitler came to power, and had been written before. The death penalty for shipping money out of the Reich came at the end of 1936. Nazi espionage in banks came later yet.[20] Swiss banking secrecy was not meant for Jews, and there is no evidence that it affected Jews especially.

The second myth is pernicious because it follows Nazi (and Communist) propaganda so closely. According to it, the Jews had gathered up a disproportionate amount of old Europe's wealth. As soon as things started getting hot for them, they transferred it to a central location, Switzerland, from which they hoped economically to recolonize their old areas once the danger was past. So, the story goes, the people who died in places like Auschwitz more likely than not had Swiss bank accounts and insurance policies.

Worse than nonsense. The equation of Jews with wealth and mobile capitalism holds only at the margin (and a low margin it is) for the relatively small number of Jews in Western Europe—not at all for the numerous, poor denizens of Eastern *shtetels*. The notion that the wealth of Europe was in Jewish hands—and that the Jews saw the Nazis' danger soon enough to safeguard their wealth but too late to protect themselves—is an implausible falsehood made to justify anti-Semitism.

Moreover, even if the second myth were true, it does not follow that the clever, capitalist Jews would have safeguarded their assets in Switzerland. New York was protected by the Atlantic, London by the English Channel, Paris by the Maginot Line and the world's most prestigious army. Switzerland was protected by what? Neutrality? The Alps? Let us be serious. Remember, Switzerland has only its back to the Alps. Germany essentially had an unfettered path if it chose to invade. And it is difficult to imagine that the Nazis would have respected Swiss neutrality out of respect for international law. That is why the Belgians put their gold in Paris, and the Swiss themselves put their gold in New York and London. Anyone who thought Zurich safer than these was not so smart.

And yet uncritical acceptance of these myths is the basis of the most official position of the U.S. government, the so-called Eizenstat report of 1997. The opening paragraph of the relevant section reads: "There were ample reasons to believe that Swiss banks and insurance companies held the assets of many Jewish and non-Jewish victims." The impression the text means to convey by the word "many" is that there were more such assets in Switzerland than anywhere else. But the authors do not cite these "ample reasons" and dare not make the claim explicitly, because it is insupportable. "Moreover, it was believed by many Jewish organizations and the Allies that the other neutrals would not have significant amounts of heirless assets." But why delimit the field to the neutrals? Why not make comparisons with France, Britain, and the United States, which is where smart money was likeliest to flee? "Switzerland introduced bank secrecy in part to counter Nazi efforts to block or trace capital outflows from Germany into Swiss banks." But there was no capital outflow from Germany at the time Switzerland introduced bank secrecy, much less were there Nazi efforts to counter it. Why would historians write things so patently untrue? "In the 1930s it made sense for any European who feared political unrest, confiscation, or war to protect family assets by placing them in Switzerland." It may have made sense according to the flawed facts and logic of the Eizenstat report, but it certainly did not make sense to the Belgians, Dutch, and Swiss governments, all Europeans, who in fact put their money elsewhere.

One would have expected the Eizenstat report, whose purpose was to explore the issue of heirless accounts, to provide some facts about the number and value of such accounts, as well as facts about how access to those accounts had been managed and perhaps how it should have been managed. But no. A document of 49 preface pages and 208 main text pages contains only 16 on its ostensible subject—heirless assets in Switzerland. And those pages contain *not one solitary fact* about how many victims of Nazism put how much money where or what happened to it. Rather, those 16 pages chronicle communications between Switzerland and the United States about their respective laws on the subject.

Nonetheless, the tone of the report strongly suggests that Switzerland, a Nazi sympathizer and collaborator, took the Jews' money just as it took Nazi gold, and got away with it for a long time—but that the day of reckoning was at last at hand.

The point, in short, was to extort money from the Swiss. As in the days of Brennus, and World War II, and as ever it shall be, when the sword is heavy, the arguments don't have to be good, or the scales honest.

CHAPTER 5

Money and Power in U.S. Foreign Policy

"The strong do what they can and the weak suffer what they must."

—Thucydides

B ETWEEN 1995 AND 1999 SWITZERLAND was again beset by a great power's claim on its economy. The challenge posed by the Clinton administration and the World Jewish Congress had one element in common with that of World War II: Power alone determined how much the weak had to pay to the strong. The power was wielded by American public figures acting officiously rather than officially on behalf of private parties, while the ransom was paid by Swiss private parties to satisfy a claim that had been made on the whole country. Why? Because the American private parties had access to just a bit of the power of the U.S. government.

It hardly matters how Edgar Bronfman, president of the World Jewish Congress (WJC), rented the governmental power he wielded against Switzerland. The point is that the money he invested in political contributions within the U.S. political system ended up delivering to him control over a disproportionately larger amount of money. It was domestic interest–group politics projected internationally. Power makes money.

By September 1995, when Edgar Bronfman met with the president of Switzerland and had lunch with the Swiss Bankers' Association, his hosts knew that his WJC was demanding money. The WJC had already shown that it could embarrass the president of Austria, Kurt Waldheim, by generating media attention about his wartime collaboration with Nazi abuses. In Eastern Europe the WJC had taken the lead in a drive to return former Jewish property—mostly old synagogue buildings—to Jewish use. And it had already fired a shot across Switzerland's bow by generating articles that publicized a long-standing fact: Swiss banks still carried many accounts that had not been claimed since the war, and Jews claiming to be heirs of depositors had received little help and much insensitivity from the banks. Therefore, the articles generated by the WJC suggested, the banks were perpetuating at least part of one of the century's most disgraceful episodes—and hinted at a broader critique of Switzerland's role in the war.[1]

Swiss authorities, and the bankers themselves, were eager enough to pay in order to avoid having to defend themselves against these charges. In 1962, and again in 1995, the government had ordered the banks to search for accounts *that might be construed as having belonged to foreign Jews.* Since there is no way of knowing for sure the relationship of any given account holder to the Nazi regime or to its victims, never mind the holder's race or religion, the number and amount they came up with each time necessarily depended on arbitrary criteria for designating an account holder as "Jewish" in his or her absence. The 1962 survey picked out as Jews some 750 persons who had Jewish-sounding names. The 1995 survey started from the opposite premise: unless there was reason to think otherwise, the account was dubbed "Jewish." The 1995 surveys had indicated that eight hundred accounts still unclaimed after previous reviews contained approximately $32 million. The Swiss bankers were eager to give this sum to Mr. Bronfman (sixty-four times what the Kennedy administration had given to Jewish organizations in 1962), and to be left alone. So, at the lunch, they formally offered it to the WJC. Bronfman did not even consider the offer; his interest, he claimed, lay in setting up a process to determine just how much was owed.

The Swiss authorities and bankers had no idea of the power that Bronfman represented, or of what he would put them through. They also held on to the silly notion that Bronfman was interested only in the money in unclaimed accounts. In fact, since Bronfman never advanced objective criteria for his demands, he wanted such money as his power could reap. The fuss over the unclaimed accounts and the banks' well-known insensitive insistence that claimants provide full documentation for their claim was only a kind of propellant for a much bolder claim on the whole of Switzerland for alleged past sins. Just as his claims went beyond what might be called justice for individual Jews, Bronfman's power was rooted not so much in the Jewish community as in the American political process itself.

Bronfman and the WJC

Edgar Bronfman describes his life as a love-hate relationship with his father's legacy.[2] In his book, *The Making of a Jew*, he recounts that as a college student his first act of rebellion was to abandon Judaism *de facto*. But because of family and business connections, he still moved in Jewish circles and fulfilled his father's role in Jewish charities. Nahum Goldmann, president of the World Jewish Congress, recognized Bronfman's business talents; in 1979 he drew Bronfman into succeeding him as president of the WJC, then at a low point of influence.

The WJC had been founded in Geneva in 1936 to marshal the efforts of Jewish organizations around the world to induce their respective governments to accept Jews fleeing Nazism. It failed. After the war, it succeeded in becoming the broker of a settlement between Ben Gurion's Israel and Adenauer's Germany that eventually yielded Israel $73 billion. This success came because the state of Israel chose the WJC as an intermediary, and Adenauer's Germany was eager to pay. Success did not come from any strength inherent in the congress. In short, the WJC is an organization of organizations that has tried to cast itself as the representative of all the world's Jews. In this it has not been terribly successful; the state of Israel, home to about one-third of the world's Jewish population, does not delegate the right to represent world Jewry, more than a third of all Jews live in the United States and think of themselves as part of other organizations or none at all, while the rest are scattered over the rest of the world and wield little influence. The power of the WJC, therefore, has waxed and waned with the willingness of governments to give it a role.

As regards the anti-Swiss campaign, and contrary to its claims, the WJC emphatically did not act as an agent of the state of Israel. Interviewed by this author, responsible officials in Jerusalem's Foreign Ministry, who requested anonymity, stated that it was not Israel's position that Switzerland had collaborated with the Nazis during World War II, that the state of Israel was not a party to the WJC's campaign, and that it wanted to stay as far away from that campaign as possible. Israel, they said, had better relations with Switzerland than with any other European country. Relations were particularly close between the two countries' armed forces since they were the only ones in the world based to the maximum extent on reserves. Israel would do nothing to jeopardize these relations. When asked whether Israel would agree to distribute any of the money from the settlement between the WJC and Switzerland, one official recoiled in horror, while the other said that regardless of how much trouble such a task would make for Israel, the government could not refuse it if the WJC offered. But both agreed that Bronfman would never make such an offer. In short, Israel's position is that the World Jewish Congress in no way represents Israel.

Bronfman increased the WJC's power by raising money, and his own by buying access to government with his own and his company's political contributions. He also had a flair for picking causes and for making bold assertions of authority. In the 1980s the congress rose to prominence by championing the cause of Jews in the old Soviet Union. Bronfman's small measure of success in this came because he pressed the idea onto Soviet leaders that earning a clean bill of health from Jewish businessmen was the road to getting what they wanted from the West. Under Bronfman, the WJC has also worked to build up Jewish education in order to strengthen Jewish identity and discourage assimilation.

Bronfman makes clear that his effort in such causes was not because he had become either a believer or a practitioner of Judaism. Rather, mild curiosity about the religion resulted from his success in building the WJC's organization. He wrote that he began to read a little of the Bible for the first time in 1994. He got the identity he had sought from childhood from his secular, organizational involvement in Jewish causes.

The depth of Bronfman's identity as a Jew may be seen by his non-liquor business, namely entertainment. Seagram Company bought Interscope Records, which produced CDs of "gangsta rappers" and such disciples of pornography, violence against women, and death as Marilyn Manson and Nine Inch Nails. Until August 1997 Bronfman also owned Death Row Records, which produced the equally deadly works of rappers Tupac Shakur and Snoop Doggy Dogg. He sold the latter only under pressure from shareholder lawsuits. Since no moral code, certainly not Judaism, sanctions such things, it is safe to conclude that morality did not drive Edgar Bronfman. His anti-Swiss campaign had nothing to do with religion, and little to do with race. It was personal fulfillment through the exercise of power.

Power

Bronfman's power consisted of high-level connections within the Democratic Party, of which he was a principal financier in New York and California, as well as at the national level.

A measure of that power is the Bronfman family's (and company's) 1995–1996 soft money donation of $1,261,700 to the Clinton-Gore campaign. Throughout the country, countless local Democratic officials know that pleasing Bronfman means money, as well as favor in Washington. As the Eizenstat report's reference to President Clinton suggests, the president himself ordered Undersecretary of State Stuart Eizenstat to put the State Department's resources behind Bronfman's effort to get money from the Swiss. Such Democratic officeholders as New York City Comptroller Alan Hevesi and then California Lieutenant Governor Gray Davis did not need much prompting to follow Bronfman's lead.

Occasionally Bronfman's money lures Republicans. For the anti-Swiss campaign Bronfman was able to recruit Alfonse D'Amato, then Republican senator from New York and chairman of the Senate Banking Committee. D'Amato had already earned a reputation for wholehearted devotion to his constituents' claims, becoming known as "Senator Pothole," and sending out his staff on what he called "pork patrols" to discover any and all benefits for his constituents. From his beginnings as a politician on Long Island, D'Amato had developed sincere affection for the two dominant ethnic groups of his area, the Italians and the Jews. One photo in his office showed him bowing under the pope's extended hand, and another next to former Israeli Prime Minister Menachem Begin (and indistinguishable from him). He never looked too closely at the merits of the claims of his favorite groups but took on their causes with gusto. Of all the politicians involved in Bronfman's effort against Switzerland, D'Amato may have been the only one who actually believed the whole set of accusations. None of this kept Bronfman from helping Charles Schumer, a wheelhorse of New York's Democratic Party machine, in his successful 1998 campaign to unseat Senator D'Amato.

When Bronfman approached Swiss bankers and officials, he had reason to believe that a campaign in the press and pressure from the Clinton administration would be enough to shake a multibillion-dollar sum out of the Swiss government. But it quickly became clear that while such weapons could generate pressure, they could not actually force the Swiss to pay. Thus as early as 1996 Bronfman turned to what had become the routine, profitable way to fleece politically weak corporate enemies in America—the class action lawsuit. A few words are in order on this feature of latter-day American public life.

Until 1966 plaintiffs who wanted to join in a common, class action lawsuit against a company had actually to co-sign the same documents. As a result, participants in such suits were few. Their specific interest made it likely that they, rather than their lawyers, would keep control of the suit and its proceeds. That year, however, a new law allowed some plaintiffs to claim that they were representing all actual or potential plaintiffs similarly affected by the defendant. Industry did not object too strenuously because this allowed a judge to foreclose any suit by any individual deemed to have been a member of the "class" whose representatives the judge had previously recognized. So, in a way, the law allowed defendants to make one-time payments for protection against lawsuits.

Since 1966 any person who wants *not* to be part of a class action suit either because he wishes to preserve his own right to sue or because he does not feel represented by those whom the judge has recognized as representatives of the class must file an affidavit stating why he is not part of the class. But this rarely happens. Hence the "classes" contain huge numbers who wind up with pittances. The parties who gain the most money are the lawyers who bring the suits. The politicians who back them gain power as well as some cash.

This system has put great power in the hands of judges. If the judge finds that any given set of plaintiffs (in practice, their lawyers) represents a class containing millions of people, the lawyers for that class can bring enormous pressure to bear on the defendant to settle—meaning to pay ransom without ever going to trial. The suits are usually brought by public officials, or ostentatiously backed by them. Tearful "victims" make good subjects for the evening news, which begins the pressure on corporate targets. In the lengthy process of fighting the suits through innumerable legal maneuvers, the defendants stand to gain nothing if they win and to lose much regardless of whether they win or lose, while the plaintiffs' lawyers lose nothing but their time if the suit fails and stand to make fortunes if it succeeds. Then there is the process of "discovery," by which the defendants' documents are used to generate unfavorable headlines. And of course, as in the Swiss case, the judges themselves put pressure on the defendants to settle by letting them know how they would rule. But the real hammer is that public officials take the presence of the class action suits they themselves are generating, or backing, as an excuse to act as if all the plaintiffs' accusations had been proven. Thus they begin to issue bureaucratic regulations, hold up licenses, and generally harass the defendants. So much for the "stick." The "carrot" in class action suits is the defendant's expectation that once a settlement is reached with the officially sanctioned claimants, the settlement will preclude other challenges. Indeed, in the multi-billion-dollar settlement by state attorneys general against U.S. tobacco companies, the government pledged special protection of the defendants' market share and profits. This guaranteed a steady stream of cash for the plaintiffs while the defendants pass to consumers the cost of buying protection both from government and from competitors. In other words, the process amounts to using the legal system to run a protection racket.

The truth of the accusations is immaterial, above all because those who bring the suits have every intention of preventing them from coming to trial before a jury. In the words of Andrew Cuomo, President Clinton's secretary of housing and urban development, gun manufacturers would be subjected to the "death of a thousand cuts" if they resisted pressure to accept his demands. But, "If all the parties act in good faith we'll stay at the negotiating table."[3] Cuomo was referring to a suit he brought supposedly on behalf of public housing tenants alleging that gun manufacturers had been negligent as regards sales and safety devices and hence were responsible for the fact that residents of federal housing projects were several times more likely to be shot than the average American. The suit was backed by President Clinton himself, for whom reduction in gun ownership by Americans has been a goal put out of reach by the public's opposition. But a straightforward trial of the accusations would not have brought Cuomo and Clinton closer to their goal. Any trial would have shown their allegation to be a *non sequitur*, that the manufacturers' behavior followed existing law, and that some public housing tenants' appetite for crack cocaine fed drug traffickers and their violence. Such suits are no more about law than about truth, however; they are about who can do what to whom.

Often, as in a major suit against the makers of women's silicone breast implants, research eventually shows that the accusations are scientifically groundless. Never mind. By then the defendants have "settled," giving up the right to sue back. And lots of money has changed hands. The real-life "heroine" of the blockbuster movie *Erin Brockovich* made $2 million out of accusations against a California utility for its disposal of a chemical that she claimed caused many diseases. Later it was proved that the chemical in question in the concentrations cited was unlikely to have caused any of them. No matter. The take was $333 million.

This is very big business. Some law firms involved in a massive suit against U.S. tobacco companies in the 1990s netted billion-dollar chunks of the $246 billion settlement spread out over twenty-five years. In Texas alone, the lawyers' take was

$3 billion. These lawyers, collectively known as the "Plaintiff Bar," then recycle some of their profits to the Democratic politicians who make the suits possible. A tobacco suit lawyer who contributed $70,000 said: "We want to make sure we have a Democratic president, House, and Senate. There is some serious tobacco money being spread around."[4] In 1999 the top five law firms that benefited from the tobacco suits recycled $1.8 million of "soft money" into the Democratic Party. In the 1996 election cycle, trial lawyers contributed some $5 million in soft money to the party and another $5 million in money to specific Democratic candidates. Thus they are one of the party's top constituencies. By comparison, note that Bronfman, his company, and his family contributed some $1.25 million.

Settlements also end typically with the defendants' agreeing with some of the accusations, as well as with the regulations slapped on their activities that the officials sought in the first place but were unable to achieve through the legislative process. In the domestic arena class action suits have become perhaps the principal means by which the Democratic Party and its associated interest groups achieve political goals, penalize their political opponents, and take in money—all things they could not do by passing laws or trying cases.

Since corporations pass the cost of class action lawsuits on to the customers as part of the cost of doing business, such suits end up taxing some citizens for the benefit of others—specifically for the benefit of the Democratic Party and its constituents. Unsurprisingly, the most successful combination in the field of class action suits has been between federal officials—almost always Democrats—and state and local Democratic Party officials, preeminently Democratic state attorneys general as well as lawyers associated with the Democratic Party. During the late 1990s this practice became so closely identified with the Democratic Party that Republican state attorneys general formed their own association and increasingly refused to take part in class action suits. In the Swiss case the class action suits aimed at taxing a whole foreign country on behalf of a constituency of the U.S. Democratic Party.

Note that class action suits without trial, which some of their practitioners defend as a way of tackling social problems despite a gridlocked political system,[5] are essentially private actions made possible by access to public power, both judicial and executive. They cut ordinary voters out of decisions on public policy as well as about taxes.[6] They are also actions by public officials acting as private citizens but with all the advantages of public office. The ostensibly voluntary settlements in which these suits end absolve public officials of responsibility for their actions on behalf of the plaintiffs because, after all, the parties themselves "agreed" to the deal. These trials of power are unalloyed by the responsibilities of public office.

For Edgar Bronfman's campaign against Switzerland, the class action suit was the likeliest means of actually ensuring that some Swiss would pay. That is because even in the 1990s there was a limit to the power that the U.S. government, or any government, could exercise over a foreign country without taking official action. All the Swiss government had to do was call the U.S. government's bluff. Was the Clinton administration really ready to explain to Congress and the American people why they ought to treat Switzerland as an enemy? The Swiss don't make very convincing villains. The roughly five hundred American companies that have operations in Switzerland would probably not have cooperated with any of the Clinton administration's unofficial calls for an economic boycott because they would have been hurt by Swiss retaliation. Could any major American company have been pressured into joining sanctions against the Swiss? Not likely. So, since dragging the American people as a whole into a confrontation with the Swiss was never an option, concrete pressures would be limited to what Democratic officials could do without taking actions that would expose them to public opposition. Through purely discretionary power, Democratic officials could have disinvested state government retirement funds in Swiss banks and companies. Although this was small stuff, it would have exposed these funds' managers to the ire of contributors whose accounts would have been hurt.

As for the Swiss government, however willing it might have been to pay the kind of money that Bronfman demanded, its hands would have been tied by the sort of national referendum that always accompanies major decisions in Switzerland.

Given these difficulties, the campaign could be sure of "closing the deal" only if it could actually cause so much trouble for some Swiss company in the United States that the company would conclude that settling was the cheapest alternative. That is why Bronfman needed a means of pulling the campaign entirely within U.S. borders and into a friendly venue. The class action suit became the weapon of choice. As with domestic class action suits, the amount of the settlement would be just a bit less than what would lead the defendant to go out of business or to fight.

The practical difficulties were disposed of quickly. The WJC had nothing but contempt for the plaintiffs' lawyers who had been working up suits against the Swiss. It nevertheless entered the suits because they were the ideal vehicle. For their part, the plaintiffs' lawyers distrusted the WJC but realized that it could bring to bear the pressure of public officials who were beyond the reach of the lawyers themselves.

Three sets of lawyers brought the original formal suits. In the eastern district of New York the cases were *Weisshaus et al.* v. *Union Bank of Switzerland et al.* plus four others; the northern district of California saw *Markorivikova et al.* v. *Swiss Bank Corporation et al.*; and *Rosenberg* v. *Swiss National Bank* was filed in the district court for the District of Columbia. Formally, the WJC was only an "organizational endorser," and as such it signed the settlement agreement. But because it had superior political connections it also negotiated the agreement and had the major influence in the all-important distribution of the proceeds. Moreover, the Swiss side began to pay attention to the suits only when the WJC joined them, because only Bronfman's connections with American politicians could make real trouble for them, and only the same politicians who were behind the trouble could come close to guaranteeing that the first payoff would be the last.

In sum, power in the end game turned out to lie not so much in direct diplomatic support from the Clinton administration, in the press reports generated by Senator Alfonse D'Amato, or in the Eizenstat report. Rather, it lay in the existence of a vulnerable target company within U.S. borders, and of a judge who would accept his plaintiffs' breathtaking claim to be *the* representatives of countless victims of the Holocaust. Above all it depended on Democratic New York City Comptroller Alan G. Hevesi, who could impose upon the company costs far greater than Bronfman's demands.

Hevesi, whose family in Hungary had been decimated in the Holocaust, was a lifelong supporter of Jewish causes. He was also the epitome of Democratic Party careerism. First elected to the New York State Assembly in 1971 from the borough of Queens, Hevesi became the assembly's Democratic whip in 1978. After unsuccessful attempts to advance in state government, Hevesi was elected city comptroller in 1993 when a corruption scandal forced New York's Democratic Party to drop its first choice, Elizabeth Holtzman. In office, Hevesi sought to build credits within the party and with its donors to become the Democratic nominee to succeed New York City Mayor Rudolph Giuliani. His actions in the Swiss case improved his prospects.

A Suit Grows in Brooklyn

The venue of the WJC's suit against the Swiss banks was not chosen at random. No venue for a class action suit is left to chance. Making sure the right judge is in charge of a case is a high art. Although friendly judges abounded in Washington, D.C., California, and elsewhere, the main effort was in Brooklyn, New York. The city is the world's financial center. It is also a place where nearly all officials somehow depend for their careers on the Democratic Party. Not incidentally, New York has more Jews than Tel Aviv. But why Brooklyn rather than Manhattan? The federal judge in Brooklyn, Edward Korman, was a reliable ally. Korman himself was a Democrat, appointed to the federal bench through the patronage ("senatorial courtesy") of New York's Democratic senator, Daniel Patrick Moynihan, who followed the priorities of Brooklyn's very tight Democratic organization.

That organization's workings came to national attention in 1999–2000, after two local lawyers decided they had not received their proper cut of patronage from the Kings County (Brooklyn) courthouse. The lawyers turned over to state officials (who then brought in the FBI) details of how Brooklyn's Democratic Party controls the appointment of judges, who then hand out lucrative administrative assignments to lawyers who support the Democratic Party. A party insider described these revelations as "radioactive."[7] But the only thing new about the revelations of partisan corruption was that former insiders had made them publicly. That judges in Brooklyn at all levels are selected and work as part of a corrupt party machine has been an open secret for a century.

Unsurprisingly, Judge Korman accepted the non-self-evident contention of the plaintiffs and the World Jewish Congress that they represented vast classes of individuals victimized by the Swiss banks and government—an assertion that the plaintiffs made no effort to document. The judge left the details of the nature of the class, and of the plaintiff's precise relationship with the class, to be worked out as part of the settlement. In other words he allowed the plaintiffs to pursue a campaign of pressure, one result of which would be that the defendants would be forced to agree to the plaintiffs' right to exert the pressure. Judge Korman managed not to express any substantive judgment on either the claim of representation or the substance of the charge. But what he did was enough.

Here is how the banks were made to pay. On December 14, 1997, Undersecretary Eizenstat convened a meeting in Zurich with Switzerland's top bankers, the WJC's Israel Singer, and the plaintiffs' lawyers. Three facts dominated the meeting. First, the Swiss public's increasingly outraged reaction at the campaign made it inconceivable that the Swiss government would meet the Americans' demands. If the demands were to be met, the banks would have to do it. Second, a week earlier Alan Hevesi had gathered like-minded state and local officials, including many Democratic state treasurers, at New York's Plaza Hotel. The meeting had authorized sanctions (such as withholding licenses and disinvesting in Swiss banks) if the Swiss did not pay. Hevesi had required executives of the main Swiss banks doing business in New York to face this hostile audience. Third, Undersecretary Eizenstat and the Clinton administration feared that the confrontation they had helped set up between their U.S. clients and Switzerland was spiraling into a real international crisis. This could force Clinton to choose between stranding his domestic clients or fighting a battle that the American public would likely disavow. Therefore Eizenstat convened the meeting to broker a settlement.

Although the Swiss bankers were willing to pay, they discussed only sums somehow tied to the dormant accounts. After all, it seemed to them that this is what the fuss was about, and that is why they had agreed to pay for a massive audit of their bank records headed by former U.S. Federal Reserve Chairman Paul Volcker to determine the outer limits of the value of such accounts. What was the point of the Volcker inquiry if they were to pay an amount unrelated to it? But the fuss was not really about the accounts. So, no deal.

The two sides met again, in January 1998, in Eizenstat's State Department office. The U.S. government's participation in private suits had been anathema to American law, based as it is on the distinction between public and private, as well as on official impartiality in private disputes. But Eizenstat, using the influence of his position in the Clinton administration, pressured the Swiss side to negotiate a settlement unrelated to the amount in the dormant accounts. Later, Eizenstat argued that he had acted to bring about "justice."[8] Friends of Eizenstat say that his breach of American legal practice had been for the sake of sparing the Swiss the worst consequences of "a crazy American legal system."

The Swiss got the message that they would have to pay an amount unrelated to any objective criterion, and in return asked that any amount agreed upon serve to immunize their banks and their country against further suits. The budding agreement, however, was nipped by the arrival of the WJC's Israel Singer, who managed to anger both the plaintiffs' lawyers and the Swiss with high demands backed by the specter of what his friend Alan Hevesi could do. In subsequent meetings, Singer would bring Hevesi along because, he said, "I didn't want to be shooting blanks."[9]

And indeed Hevesi was shooting live ammo. If the banks had not agreed to a settlement, his committee would apply sanctions against Switzerland. More important, he himself would act to deny the operating license for the merger of the Union Bank of Switzerland and Swiss Bank Corporation, which would create UBS, Europe's largest bank. Hevesi had set March 26, 1998, as the deadline. On March 24 he formally objected to the merger, due to take place in July. These banks have hugely profitable operations in New York—some $4 billion per year. Had the two banks not been merging and thus had they not needed a new license, bringing pressure against them would have required moving against existing licenses, something that would have required much more exposure on the part of judges and officials. But in fact Hevesi could bring enormous pressure to bear simply by opposing the new license.

This put Stuart Eizenstat and the Clinton administration in a bind. Foreign policy is supposed to be the exclusive responsibility of the federal government. But now, a city official and like-minded fellow Democrats were about to start a real economic war that was sure to be more trouble for the Clinton administration than the support of the lawyers and Jewish organizations was worth. And it was a war that the Clinton administration had primed them for, albeit unofficially.

Eizenstat went to New York to try to damp the fire he had done so much to start. At this point the banks could have made a powerful bargaining chip out of the contrast between the Clinton administration's intense desire to avoid an international incident and the substantial unity of Swiss public opinion. But by this time the banks were thoroughly spooked. On March 26 the Swiss formally agreed to Eizenstat's proposal that they stop insisting on merely paying out sums related to the dormant accounts and instead negotiate a higher, comprehensive, "rough justice" amount unrelated to any datum. In exchange for that agreement, Alan Hevesi held off sanctions until June 30. But since he had already objected to the scheduled July merger, he had set up the biggest possible sanction, one that would cost the banks 300 million francs per month.

As the talks moved back to Eizenstat's State Department office, the Swiss government announced that it would not contribute to the settlement. The last public policy connection had fallen away. Now the issue had come down to how much the two banks would pay for the U.S. Democratic Party's permission to do business. In his U.S. government office, but of course unofficially, Eizenstat suggested that the Jewish groups' demands of $1.8 billion and the Swiss offer of $300 million be reconciled at $1.25 billion. On June 30, on Eizenstat's advice, Hevesi formally dropped his objection to the merger. But when the Swiss banks' final offer came in at only $530 million, he angrily vowed to resume the objection. Also, beginning in September, Hevesi's committee of state officials would disinvest from all Swiss companies the state pension funds they managed. But by then the banks had long since given up thoughts of fighting.

The final act began when Judge Korman—could he possibly have felt the Clinton administration's pain?—invited all parties to dinner near his courthouse, where he asked both sides to outline the case that each would make in a trial. No one doubted that this was in fact *the* trial, though unencumbered by rules or responsibility. Having heard the arguments, Korman advised the defendants that the courts could possibly make them pay far more than what they had offered, and the plaintiffs that conceivably none of their evidence might be admissible in the federal court system—especially in courts of appeal. Since he would have a lot to say about what evidence would be allowed and what amount would be set, he was not "shooting blanks" either. Then he suggested a settlement figure of $1.25 billion. Perhaps serendipitously, this was exactly as much as Eizenstat had suggested. The two sides got the message, and on August 12, 1998 they settled on that figure.

Once the banks, the WJC, and the plaintiffs' lawyers had seen the wisdom of the Clinton administration's recommendation, Alan Hevesi ceased to have trouble with the license. The threat of sanctions evaporated quicker than it had materialized. Officially, Hevesi, Judge Korman, the Senate, and even the Clinton administration had done *nothing*. No votes were recorded, no formal accusations made, no formal actions were taken, no judgment on evidence was made. Everything was done officiously.

So, the resolution of the anti-Swiss campaign came down to the mundane capacity of officials to use public offices for private purposes informally to force private party "B" to pay their friends in private party "A." In January 1999, as the banks were setting about paying $1.25 billion over three years—just under 10 percent of profits—Richard Capone of the now merged UBS mused how much cheaper it would have been to buy influence in New York's ruling Democratic Party, just as businesses do with ruling parties in much of the world: "But it never occurred to me that in America we would have to pay bribes."[10]

Clean Hands

Bribes? On January 26, 1999, Melvyn I. Weiss, lawyer for one of the plaintiffs, declared in court: "Don't ever let the Swiss government get away with saying they are absolved because of this."[11] But absolution is precisely what the settlement agreement says that the defendants bought for $1.25 billion. Judge Korman's provisional acceptance of the settlement agreement closed the five cases in his court. Plaintiffs' lawyers in Brooklyn were able to guarantee that the settlement would also cover the cases in California and the District of Columbia. This showed that the individuals in whose names those suits had been brought had been mere pawns. Nevertheless, although it was certain that the banks would pay money to organizations, it was by no means sure what those organizations would do with the money or even what the banks payments would exempt them, or Switzerland, from.

The agreement began by laying out the plaintiffs' allegations: Switzerland collaborated with the Nazi regime and unlawfully participated "in a scheme" to retain class members' accounts. The Swiss also dealt in looted assets. They profited from slave labor because the Reich's economy during the war depended in part on slave labor, economic resources were fungible, and Nazi Germany deposited in Switzerland some of its proceeds. Finally, the Swiss tried to cover up their role. Then the agreement stated that the Swiss side did not agree with the allegations, that each side believed that it could uphold its case in court, but that both had chosen the settlement instead: $1.25 billion would purchase the end of the anti-Swiss campaign and preclude further suits relating to World War II. The court stated that it was taking no position with regard to either side's claims, and that it was not about to argue with the parties' agreement—*it had nothing to do with it*. This, of course, was insincere.

On March 30, 1999, the court issued an "Order Preliminarily Approving Material Terms of the Proposed Class Action Settlement Agreement and Provisionally Certifying the Proposed Settlement Classes." This document further distanced the court from the substance of the accusations and of the agreement by stating at length that the plaintiffs' claim to representation was not "wholly unreasonable" (maybe a little unreasonable?) and lay within the legal boundaries of class action suits. In this regard the document did not go beyond stating that the settlement fell "within the range of possible approval." What indeed that range may be, and why, the court did not attempt to say.

The document also stated that the settlement "does not disclose grounds to doubt its fairness or other obvious deficiencies, such as preferential treatment of class representatives or of segments of the class, or excessive compensation for attorneys." Yet the document did not try to define what the proper treatment of class representatives (especially the WJC) might be, nor what any segment of any class should receive. It left these questions to a "special master," whom the court would appoint within thirty days. Compensation for attorneys was also left up to the "master's" determination and the court's administrative approval at a later time. The document, in short, delegated the substance of judgment to an administrator.

Finally, the document laid out the classes into which the plaintiffs/beneficiaries were to be divided. These divisions were proper, it said, because the defendants/releasees had agreed to them. But, of course, since the defendants' only interest in the settlement concerned their release from liability, and therefore since they could not have cared less to whom the payments would go, their agreement did not justify the classes. In essence, the court ratified the results of the WJC's pressures on two Swiss banks and set the stage for distributing the proceeds according to the WJC's wishes.

On March 31, 1999, Judge Korman appointed Judah Gribetz to be the "special master" who would draw up the detailed plan to distribute and apportion attorney fees. Part of the city's Democratic machine, Gribetz was not chosen randomly any more than Korman had been. Gribetz had been a member of the Judicial Selection Committee that had "advised" Democratic Senator Moynihan on federal judicial appointments in New York State—the committee that had "advised" on Korman's job. Gribetz was also president of the Jewish Community Relations Council, a compendium of sixty New York Jewish organizations, and a longtime advocate of Jewish causes. The various parties who expected a slice of the proceeds owed much to Gribetz, and he in turn owed much to each of them. In this and in other "special masters" the power of interest groups is clothed with official authority. What began as an interest group campaign clothed first in the garb of morality and foreign policy, and then in that of a judicial proceeding, ended up as a naked interest group play once again.

Gribetz's job was to reconcile the welter of interests among groups and individuals who clamored for a slice of the proceeds. Ordered in March 1999 to submit a tentative plan for distribution by December 29 of that year, Gribetz got an extension until March 31, 2000. Judge Korman went out of his way to state that Gribetz was not especially connected with any group of claimants or lawyers: "I am not going to do anything that is going to create the reality or the impression that anyone has the inside track."[12] But since there were no objective criteria for deciding about distribution any more than there had been objective criteria for deciding the settlement amount, Gribetz's plan for distribution could only ratify the power of each party to get the inside track.

By March 14, 2000, however, Korman had issued a strange order to the effect that Gribetz would not submit his plan until further notice. Korman stated that the report must await his final ruling on the case, and that that would come only after the Swiss banks had "implement[ed] two of the central recommendations of the Volcker commission." He, not Volcker, called these matters "central." They were the creation of "a central archive of data on all 4.1 million accounts to be established and [publication of] the names of some 25,000 account holders identified as possibly or probably related to victims of Nazi persecution."

This is strange because as we shall see the Volcker report actually *discouraged* publication of massive numbers of names. Also, Israel Singer had expressed strong reservations about such publication. Nevertheless, in March 2000 Swiss bankers, perhaps looking forward to being spectators of the consequences, decided to publish the names of the accounts. The archive on 4.1 million accounts would take time to establish, and it would be quite useless for determining the validity of individual claims, because reference to this master list would duplicate the work of the Volcker commission. The Swiss banks had no interest in this matter. Yet on May 3, 2000, Switzerland's two largest banks, UBS and Credit Suisse, agreed to establish a central archive containing the 2.1 million accounts on their records opened between 1933 and 1945. (The other 2 million were spread out among hundreds of minor banks.)

As a result, Judge Korman was quoted in the press to the effect that he might soon give final approval to the settlement and—more to the point—to the special master's report. At this writing the special master's report had not been published, much less approved. Why at least a fifteen-month delay? Why a court document giving the implausible impression that the Swiss banks, having agreed to give up $1.25 billion, were eager to hold on to the last possible scrap of the victims' money? Perhaps the answer had to do with the intensity of the fight for the money amongst the plaintiffs.

Reality: The Scramble for the Money

The battle for the $1.25 billion was between competing groups of lawyers and numerous Jewish organizations. At the court hearings on the settlement, various people had asked emotionally that the money, all of it, be distributed forthwith to Jewish and other survivors of the Holocaust, most of whom were fast approaching the natural end of their lives. Yet there was never any chance that the court would divide the settlement sum by the number of Holocaust survivors and other potential claimants, some half million people, and cut checks for $2,000 to each. This would have deprived the WJC of the power that comes from distributing a ten-figure amount of money, and the lawyers from collecting on their claims for $13 million in fees. Nor, for the same reason, was there any chance that the money would be turned over to the U.S. (or Israeli) government to be distributed under the scrutiny to which democratic governments are subject.

The interests of the individual survivors were represented by Gizella Weisshaus, in whose name attorney Edward D. Fagan had filed one of the original suits. Estranged from Fagan, she demanded that at least 70 percent of the funds go to individuals. The lawyers split into two groups, one led by Fagan, the other by Melvyn Weiss and Michael Hausfeld. Both groups of lawyers argued for their own big fees and maintained that substantial amounts of money should go to the organizations they represented, such as the Simon Wiesenthal Center in Los Angeles. Bronfman's WJC argued that it should take the lead in distributing the proceeds since, it said, Bronfman was also president of the Jewish Restitution Organization, which was connected to (but note, not under the direction of) the Israeli government. The WJC claimed that it was empowered by the state of Israel "to represent the Jewish people in Holocaust-related matters," and that "we have been mandated to represent them."[13] This was simply untrue.

Name-calling quickly came to characterize the jostling at the money trough. Columnist Charles Krauthammer said the lawyers and organizations fighting for the money "recall the worst of racial hustling and class action opportunism in the United States."[14] Abraham Foxman of the Anti-Defamation League—uninvolved in the struggle—warned that the claimants were making "an industry on the memory of the victims." And it is indeed difficult to disagree with what each of the claimants said of the others—namely, that they were chiefly interested in gaining wealth, power, and glory in the name of the dead. One lawyer charged $5,000 for reading a book on Swiss gold transactions, but this was far less damning than that under the WJC's proposal direct payments to survivors *and services provided by Jewish organizations*, however the organizations might define them, were lumped in a single category to which 80 percent of the funds would go. The rest would go straight to the organizations. But of course giving money to organizations that claim to serve survivors is more like giving money to organizations than to survivors. And in fact the structure of the settlement agreement was stacked in favor of organizations.

Of the five categories of beneficiaries established by the settlement agreement the one with the highest priority for payment, the one at first sight likeliest to deliver money to real Holocaust survivors and heirs, is comprised of those who "had assets ... on deposit at any Swiss bank, investment fund, or another custodian prior to May 9, 1945." Yet the amount of money allocated to this category could never have been more than a small slice of the $1.25 billion, and a substantial part of that slice was likely to end up in the hands of the distributing organization. By the time the Independent Committee of Eminent Persons under former Federal Reserve Chairman Paul Volcker was established to make a definitive report on the number, value, and property of accounts in Swiss banks dormant since World War II, those accounts had already been thinned by several sets of searches over the years. But while the Volcker committee examined every single account opened in Switzerland between 1933 and 1945 (6.8 million), and further increased the estimate of the number of dormant accounts that *might* have belonged to Holocaust victims, it had no more success than Swiss bankers in identifying proprietors.

The committee first excluded the accounts for which no records remained due to bank mergers and authorized disposal, as well as purely domestic accounts. It also excluded dormant accounts opened earlier (among which was one Lenin had established during his exile in Zurich). Then it matched the remaining 2.2 million accounts against the names of all known or suspected victims of the Holocaust (5.5 million). About 356,000 names matched to some extent, or were otherwise suggested to be relevant. Of these, more than 300,000 were further determined to have been domestic, or unmatched chronologically, or properly closed. Some 53,000 were left with a "possible or probable relationship with Nazi persecution." But more than half of these had been closed for various reasons, and most of the rest had been paid in some way. Only 2,726 were classified as "open and dormant." Most had little value. The Volcker report said:

> As stated earlier, identification of an account as "probably or possibly" related to a victim does not in itself indicate the validity of such a relationship. The identified accounts vary widely in the degree of probability attached to them, and there is now no way of determining the number of accounts that will be claimed or that will be recognized for payment by the claims resolution process. . . . Moreover for about half the identified accounts there is no information on account values. For accounts with such values there is little consistency in valuation dates, uncertainty as to fees and charges paid or interest credited, and the proper valuation of securities in custody accounts.[15]

The report concluded that the inclusion of any account as "probably or possibly related" is not necessarily evidence about who owns the account, since the matches involve common names, and evidence considered normal in judicial or financial proceedings is almost totally lacking. Moreover, the committee made no attempt to place monetary value on the unclaimed accounts. Thus it did not take up the bet by the Swiss bankers' association that the cost of the Volcker process—200 million Swiss francs—would exceed very substantially the amount of money it turned up.

The committee's judgment on the process of liquidating these accounts further suggested that those in charge of the process could do pretty much what they wanted:

> The experience of the Claims Resolution Tribunal [established by Swiss law in 1997] demonstrates that publication of names [of account holders] attracts multiple claimants and claims by a single claimant to numerous unrelated accounts. One danger is that a volume of frivolous claims to a very large list of published names could clog the claims resolution process, delay justice rather than serving the legitimate claimants, and introduce a substantial and undesirable element of chance into the resolution process.[16]

Certainly this had been the experience of the administrator general of Israel's Justice Ministry, who had published a list of five thousand dormant accounts held by Israeli banks and ended up giving title to all of ten claimants. Anyone whom the special master put in charge of the claims resolution process would face precisely the same problems of distribution as the Swiss banks or the Israeli justice minister had faced.

The questionnaire sent out under the court's mandate to potential claimants of these accounts asked for substantiating documents that the claimants would not be able to produce for the distributors any more than they had been able to produce for the Swiss bankers themselves. Just like the Swiss banks, the Jewish organizations would not hand out fortunes to old ladies bearing stories of a long lost father who made obscure remarks about having stashed money in a Swiss bank. Unlike the banks, however, these organizations had political constituents to feed. Besides, since the average age of potential claimants was seventy-five, they were dying off at the rate of about forty thousand per year. Hence the pressure on the distributing organizations to give away money that would otherwise be theirs was sure to diminish, while the incentive to delay would grow.

The second category, consisting of persons who lost "assets disguised by a Swiss entity for the benefit of an Axis company, entity or person associated with the Nazi regime," was even less likely to contain well-documented claims for substantial sums. How could any person whose money or business or cars were taken by the Nazis argue, much less prove, that the value of those assets was somehow "cloaked" in Switzerland rather than simply consumed in the maw of the Reich's war machine? The Volcker committee's brief reference to this problem basically stated its insolubility. The money devoted to this category also had to end up in the distributors' hands.

The third and fifth categories gave the distributors total discretion. The third concerned slave laborers whose work somehow passed through Switzerland. But to tell where the value of anyone's work flowed in a complex modern economy was as impossible as to discover what operation of a human body was due to any given bit of food it had consumed. The fifth included slave laborers who worked in Swiss-owned facilities in Nazi-occupied Europe. But by definition any factory in Germany or any occupied country operated not according to the wishes of its legal owners but according to those of the Nazis who had power of life and death over managers as well as laborers.

The fourth category, those who "unsuccessfully sought entry into Switzerland to avoid Nazi persecution," had the advantage of dealing with possibly identifiable persons. Leave aside why the plaintiffs did not seek damages against American or Swedish authorities who had denied asylum to persons fleeing the Nazis. The practical question was: How could anyone show that he or she was denied entry into Switzerland (deportation is another matter)? One person's story would be as good or as bad as another's. To the extent that refusal of asylum meant death, there should have been no one around with a right to collect. Add the fact that the distributors of the money had every reason to believe that every application they denied would mean more money for their own organization, and it was reasonable to deduce that little money from this category would ever reach individual claimants.

Who then would be the beneficiaries of such wide discretion over so much money? Could it be that past, present, and future constituents of the distributing organizations would do better than unconnected persons?

Finally, by the time of the settlement, the Jewish organizations that were vying for the power to distribute the take had compiled a solid record of delay and inefficiency in distributing previously established funds. In 1997, for example, Swiss government and industry established a $200 million fund for Holocaust victims. Distribution was to be handled by the WJC in its capacity as an affiliate of the World Jewish Restitution Organization. Yet a year after the fund was supposed to begin disbursing, the WJC had actually sent out only 10 percent of its funds. The newspapers were full of anguished cries from those who had expected benefits.[17] In the end, the effective beneficiaries turned out to be the organizations themselves. No one familiar with Michels's Iron Law of Bureaucracy could be surprised.

On the other side of the ledger, only the U.S. government could provide the two Swiss banks, and indeed Switzerland itself, with any measure of security that henceforth they would be left alone. But since the Clinton administration had never *officially* done anything to Switzerland, nor even officially threatened it with anything, it could hardly *undo* what it had not done. The Clinton administration, which had wielded a large part of the stick, had been represented in Judge Korman's courtroom by one James Gilligan, a low-ranking Justice Department lawyer who said that the settlement was "fair, reasonable, and in the public interest."[18] But the Clinton administration did not sign the document. Even if it had, the ruling of one federal court in one set of cases could not, in the strictly legal sense, prohibit other judges from entertaining similar suits. Hence the absolution that the Swiss bought was more political than legal.

And so on January 30, 1999, the U.S. and Swiss governments issued an anodyne three-paragraph "Joint Statement." It committed both countries to "strengthening and deepening the ties between our two countries in the political, economic, and cultural spheres ... [to] promote international peace and stability, ensure respect for human rights and democratic values, and encourage free markets ... to continue fighting organized crime ... [to] the exchange of people and ideas ... [and to] the further strengthening of bilateral and multilateral economic cooperation." The statement was so void of content that any student of international affairs would ask why any two governments would go through the bother of drafting it.

The answer would have to be that the two governments were burying some sort of hatchet, ending some sort of quarrel, that at least one of the two did not wish to identify. The Swiss government had every reason to identify the quarrel, and to make as clear as possible that, the price having been paid, the country could now expect to be left alone. On January 22 the Swiss Federal Council had issued a unilateral declaration that "[t]his settlement provides closure of all the financial claims raised against Switzerland." The Clinton administration, by making friendly noises void of specific references, could claim that its future intentions toward Switzerland were entirely friendly and that its hands were clean of anything that might or might not have happened in the past.

So, what the Clinton administration did to Switzerland amounted to extending abroad the American interest-group process, by which government officials purchase the support of some citizens by renting to them the power to impose costs on others. In the sixteenth chapter of *The Prince*, Niccolò Machiavelli warned rulers against this mode of governance because, he wrote, the beneficiaries would never be satisfied, and attempts to satisfy them would make opponents out of people who would not otherwise be such. The only exception to this rule, wrote Machiavelli, occurs when a government can pay off its domestic supporters with the assets of foreigners. So it might seem that when the Clinton administration filled the coffers of a valued party contributor with money taken from foreign companies, it followed Machiavelli's unexceptionable advice. But Machiavelli understood what the Clinton administration did not take into account, that when any government raids foreign citizens' or countries' assets it pays a price in international relations.

Reality: International Implications

The Clinton administration's extortion of Switzerland alienated public opinion in a historically pro-American country. Because Switzerland is a small country, some might think that the world's only superpower can afford to exchange foreigners' ill will for the satisfaction of a domestic constituency. This is not so. The United States as a whole received no benefits from the anti-Swiss campaign, yet it incurred costs.

Swiss public opinion had no reason to blame world Jewry, much less Swiss Jews, for the anti-Swiss campaign. Yet as the campaign gathered momentum and leaders of the Swiss Jewish community were not quite quick enough to disassociate themselves from it, Swiss Jews found that too many of their fellow citizens lumped them in with the "extortionists and blackmailers" of their country. This is what Swiss President Jean Pascal Delamuraz did in his 1996 departure speech. By June of 1997, when Christoph Blocher, leader of the rightist Swiss People's Party, set about mobilizing public opinion against the United States and the WJC, he was careful to absolve Swiss Jews and Jews in general from any blame for what was being done to the country. Blocher blamed "the Americans" and the Swiss political Establishment. Nevertheless, since nothing could erase the fact that the country felt itself unjustly maligned in the name and for the monetary benefit of "the Jews," Swiss Jews were left holding the proverbial bag.

Blocher intended to damage relations with the United States, and found it easy to do so. In 1992 he had led a popular movement that overturned the entire political establishment's decision to join the European Free Trade Area, a way station into the European Union. By August 1997, just five months after he had kicked off the campaign for a referendum to annul any Swiss government decision to establish a fund to pay off the WJC, observers concluded that he had won over public opinion.[19] And indeed the government was so sure it would lose the inevitable referendum that it dropped the plan. Anti-Americanism became a staple of political discourse, and books with titles such as *Switzerland's Humiliation* and *Switzerland Faced by the American Empire* enjoyed wide readership.[20]

The arguments that resonated with Swiss public opinion amounted to an indictment of the United States and of any Swiss who would take another's money to appease foreigners. How would the American people react, asked Blocher, if any European country attempted to extract money from the United States to pay alleged victims of America's war in Vietnam? How dare the Swiss government negotiate with the WJC, whose only qualification was its success in besmirching the honor of the country? How dare Americans impugn Switzerland's abstention from World War II when America itself abstained until attacked? Switzerland, too, would have fought if attacked. How dare Americans blame Switzerland for failing to take more Jewish refugees when Switzerland took more than America? And how could America accuse Switzerland of having relied on "legalisms" to survive World War II? On what else is a small country supposed to rely? Was America able to protect Switzerland? Could it ensure Switzerland's safety in the future? If not, what practical, moral, or intellectual basis· was there for its demands? And how dare America take sides with Swiss individuals of the radical left against their fellow citizens? If the Swiss Establishment wanted to pay off the Americans, let them do it with their own money, not with that of innocent Swiss citizens. Blocher's equation of America with stupid malevolence became the common currency of Swiss discourse.

While the Swiss Federal Council was propitiating the United States and feigning remorse for any sins that its fathers might have committed, Swiss public opinion was turning against both the Establishment and America.[21] Indeed, blaming the Swiss Establishment for failing to stand up to foreigners who were humiliating the country became the opposition's rallying cry. As in World War II, the government parties' understandable attempt to appease the dominant power of the day resulted in a political windfall for their opponents. In the October 1999 general election, Blocher's Swiss People's Party made the biggest gains in the history of modern Swiss politics, winning forty-four seats and becoming the country's second largest party—and perhaps its most influential. While one may debate whether this was good or bad for Switzerland, there is no doubt that for American diplomacy it was a self-inflicted wound. Nor would this be the last such wound.

No sooner was the ink dry on the Swiss settlement than the very same lawyers and organizations, backed by the very same Clinton administration, moved against Germany. It was *déjà vu* all over again. On September 11, 1998, attorney Melvyn I. Weiss filed a suit against the German steelmaker Krupp. This piggy-backed other suits filed in Judge Korman's Brooklyn courthouse (where else but Brooklyn?) against Krupp, the Ford Motor Company's branch in Germany, as well as Deutsche

Bank and German companies such as Volkswagen. The charge was that they had profited from slave labor, partly Jewish, during World War II. The *New York Times*, which had supported the anti-Swiss campaign, expressed worry that "efforts to right clear moral wrongs can be seized upon by people with less than noble motives."[22] The *Times* might have noticed this earlier. Indeed, it might have noticed that this race for a "fast buck" abroad through political influence was part and parcel of what American politics had become at home.

These suits were open to the same criticism as the anti-Swiss campaign: How can one impute profit, much less guilt, to persons who were not even born at the time the damages were done? Could anyone argue with a straight face that the prosperity of German companies in the year 2000 was due in any way to the companies' balance sheets at the end of World War II? In fact, the war's balance sheet for the German economy was total disaster. Or could one argue that any given loan by a German bank was dictated by independent judgment rather than by a *Führerbefehl*, Hitler's capricious command? It was also quite impossible to put objective value on the labor and misery inflicted on individual slave laborers during the war. The Reich enslaved perhaps 1.5 million people, of whom fewer than a quarter million remained alive in the late 1990s. Who was to distinguish rightful claimants from fraudulent ones? It was certain only that the discretionary power that would come from managing any settlement of these suits and keeping what was not distributed stood to enrich mightily the organizations and lawyers involved, and would in part find its way back into the support mechanism of the Democratic Party.

Moreover, the Third Reich had not been alone in imposing slave labor. The Soviet Union enslaved perhaps a million Germans and almost as many Poles after the war. Why were these American class action lawyers not suing Russia? Simply because Russia had neither the money nor the disposition to be blackmailed. None of this was lost on the Germans or other Europeans.

The mechanism for forcing the Germans to pay was identical to the one used against Switzerland. Once again, the Clinton administration backed the campaign through Stuart Eizenstat as well as in a meeting between President Clinton and German Chancellor Gerhard Schroeder. But, once again, the real hammer was provided by the fact that Deutsche Bank was in the process of acquiring Bankers' Trust Company in New York and needed a license from New York City Comptroller Alan Hevesi. Even after the German government agreed in principle to a multibillion-dollar settlement with the WJC, Hevesi said he would wait until the agreement was consummated before issuing the license: "The good news is that there is the beginning of an agreement to set up a process to come to a global settlement of all the remaining issues between Holocaust survivors and heirs and German institutions. In the meantime, I continue to believe that federal and state officials should take no action on the proposed merger between Deutsche Bank and Bankers' Trust until these issues are fully resolved."[23]

The deal was struck on December 17, 1999; the German government and German industry would pay $5.1 billion to "American class action lawyers and Jewish groups" in exchange for a total release from future suits.[24] Although in contrast with Switzerland there was no ambiguity about Germany's role in World War II, the softer terms of this agreement reflected the fact that Germany was more powerful vis-à-vis the United

States than was Switzerland. The sum, $5.1 billion, was less to Germany than $1.5 billion had been to Switzerland. And instead of being satisfied with an anodyne statement, the Germans demanded from the Clinton administration an official executive agreement by which the U.S. government promised to oppose any suit against Germany or German companies concerning World War II in any U.S. court. As of this writing the German government was continuing to refuse payment because the Clinton administration's proposed language for the executive order did not fully preclude further suits. Many German companies believed that the Clinton administration would be unwilling or unable to preclude such suits. By June 2000 German companies had contributed only a small percentage of their share of the fund. Also, the Germans retained the right to direct the disbursement of some of the fund. Finally, the Germans were strong enough to make public that they resented the ransom they had been forced to pay: "Ten billion marks is the final amount" that Germany will ever pay with regard to World War II, said Germany's chief negotiator, former economics minister Otto Lambsdorf.

On December 17, 1999, another group of plaintiffs' lawyers filed a nearly identical suit in Judge Korman's Brooklyn courthouse against every major bank in France, alleging that the banks had "fail[ed] to account to survivors and the families of victims for assets that were seized, blocked, or frozen and breached their contractual and fiduciary duties by failing to take reasonable steps to locate the rightful owners of these assets or their families." And in April 2000 yet another group of American lawyers filed an $18 billion suit against the Austrian government and Austrian companies for having profited from wartime slave labor. But by that time the Clinton administration had apparently decided that enough was enough and did not put the same amount of quasi-official muscle behind it.

Still, America suffered. The French did not need much prompting to try to diminish American influence wherever it could be found, and the Austrians had already made their right-most party the country's ruling party.

Ultimately, in supporting the WJC's campaign to collect money from European government and businesses in the name of Holocaust victims, President Clinton helped yield billions of francs and marks to constituents of and contributors to his own party. But the campaign yielded only negative returns for the United States as a whole. It escaped no European that the U.S. government was acting as collector for a private group. Europeans understand, better than do most Americans, the extortion of the weak by the strong and the use of foreign policy to line the pockets of domestic constituents, but they resented such things from an America that touted its morality. The anti-Swiss campaign helped convert the vast majority of Swiss and a growing number of Germans and other Europeans to the French view that America had become unbearably imperious and needed to be cut down to size. The rest of Europe asked itself when American interest groups backed by the U.S. government might come calling on them. This embittered the usual disputes over trade and foreign policy. The result was rancor mixed with disrespect.

In sum, whatever may be said of the Clinton administration's interest in supporting its constituents' claims based on the Holocaust, there is no doubt that this support abused the U.S. legal system and was a foreign policy fiasco. Worse, it taught those Americans who followed it uncritically some unrealistic notions about international affairs.

CHAPTER 6

Lessons

"Speak softly and carry a big stick."
—Theodore Roosevelt

THE U.S. GOVERNMENT'S USE OF POWER vis-à-vis Switzerland in the 1990s betrays a misconception of the role of power in international affairs; it also shows a kind of corruption of the U.S. body politic. Let us sum up the lessons of the Swiss experience in World War II and in the 1990s, first with regard to Switzerland and then to U.S. foreign policy.

Military Power is Paramount

The Swiss case recalls the timeless truth that all international requests and demands, demurrers and denials are valid only to the extent they are backed by the capacity and willingness to fight, regardless of the prospects for victory. While technical military factors such as numbers, quality of equipment, and appropriate strategy are important, the nation's bloody-minded willingness to kill and be killed is the most fundamental of factors. During World War II the several factions in Switzerland's armed forces disagreed bitterly on much. But all agreed that the *sine qua non* of their country's capacity to bargain with Nazi Germany was their willingness to wage a war that Switzerland was sure to lose. This tipped the fine balance of power and interest and made possible independence.

Switzerland's General Henri Guisan spent more time and energy on building his army's and civil society's will to sacrifice than on any other task. His orders to the army were variations on one theme: fighting to the death. His constant message to the civilian population was that the Swiss would fight for the country's honor and independence regardless of cost. He stressed that point to counter the altogether understandable sentiment in public opinion that standing up to Germany was futile. Building this foundation of military power is not necessarily the job of a military man. In Britain, Churchill did it. Guisan did it in his country because no one else was trying to do it. Creating or preserving an army's willingness to kill and be killed is the most important—and the most difficult—of military tasks. Without this willingness even the best military preparations, never mind mere military potential, are useless. Without this, the foreign policy even of large countries becomes a bluff begging to be called. Americans should have learned this lesson in Vietnam. This lesson is especially relevant at a time when many Americans who should know better tout the notion that modern technology has done away with the need for physical courage in the armed forces.

The greatest threat to a nation's military power comes from the tendency of domestic groups to identify their interest with the success of foreign powers. This leads citizens to feel greater affection for foreign causes and less enthusiasm for risking their lives for their own country. General George Washington was able to shape the whole of early America's foreign policy to smother the habit, typical of small countries, to place their hopes and fears abroad. Creating such a "national outlook" was the most militarily significant of his achievements. Keep in mind that foreign policy breeds domestic factionalism in powerful countries as well. Machiavelli reminds us that arguments about Pisa helped tear apart Renaissance Florence. Americans must not forget that the most dangerous aspect of the Cold War was that Americans' sympathy and antipathy for Communism heightened existing domestic divisions. General Guisan was not able to affect his country's foreign policy directly, but by stressing the unconditional necessity to fight for independence he succeeded substantially in creating a political atmosphere in which factionalism was hard to sustain.

This atmosphere proved to be the most effective weapon against the most dangerous kind of subversion—not the sort performed by petty agents of foreign powers, but rather the accommodationist feelings of insufficiently ardent, excessively prudent elites. Creating such an atmosphere is certainly more of a political task than a military one. And yet every military leader, as a duty to those he must order into harm's way, must somehow make sure that if there is no Churchill around, there will at least be a Guisan or a de Gaulle if not a Washington.

The indispensable element for a call to bloody duty is calling the enemy—in this case Nazi Germany—by its right name. During the battle of France there could be no dispute about who the enemy was, and thus little quarrel about the troops' duty. But between the summer of 1940 and the winter of 1943 Germany forbade Switzerland from saying out loud that the Reich was its enemy. So subversion spread beyond the "usual suspects" and became internal political decay.

The Vietnam War should have taught Americans the connection between a government's failure to identify the enemy and the enemy's capacity to broaden its appeal far beyond the "usual suspects." Presidents Kennedy and Johnson did not point to the governments of North Vietnam and the Soviet Union as evil enemies for fear of alienating the left wing of their own party. The results were predictable: The nonprofessional elements of the armed forces became less willing to expose themselves to danger. Drug use and insubordination in the services became widespread, and almost impossible to punish severely. It became illegitimate for any American to stigmatize as traitors those who were literally giving aid and comfort to the enemy that was killing fellow citizens. Most important, since the U.S. government did not forcefully counter the Soviet Union's and its allies' indictment of America and its cause in Vietnam, some mainstream Americans came to tolerate the proposition that American anti-Communists posed the greatest danger to world peace.[1] In sum, a substantial number of Americans sought their country's defeat by turning it around from within—the literal meaning of subversion. This was easier to do because the U.S. government did not publicly identify the enemy and acknowledge that America was indeed at war.

This almost happened in Switzerland in the Second World War—but did not because the army led public opinion despite all sorts of strictures.

Not least of the lessons of the Swiss experience is that, because allies are available in inverse proportion to the need for them and alliances are creatures of circumstances, military forces must not be spread out in positions where their safety depends on allies. Allies may be defeated, as France was in 1940, or fail to see their own interest, as Italy failed. Or they may be too far away to help, as America was. So Switzerland was obliged to fall back on its own resources as the storm was at its worst, and to redeploy its forces as they should have been deployed in the first place. Had the Swiss examined their military predicament and established their mountain redoubt in the sunshine of peace, the military significance of their forces would have been as sound as possible. From this firm foundation, they could have opted for the assistance of whatever allies the circumstances might have produced. But making the survival of one's military forces dependent on allies whose disposition one cannot control leads to rude awakenings.

As for neutrality, history teaches that it is the fragile creature of the balance of power, and that belligerents violate or respect neutrals' claims to the extent that either course appears to pay. Neutrality is possible only to the extent that it can be defended, and the behavior that can be expected of neutrals is proportionate to the capacity to hurt them or protect them. Both the Axis and the Allies asserted their interests vis-à-vis Switzerland proportionately to the balance of power. For either side to have pressed harder than its capacity to hurt or protect Switzerland warranted would have invited hatred as well as contempt for impotence. Had the Swiss given in to a greater extent than they had to, they would have been the contemptible ones.

Money

Governments are always under pressure from domestic groups to pay in some way for the foreign exports of domestic businesses. But when goods are sold with subsidies of any kind, the home government—that is to say the taxpayers—becomes the real payer. And the government acts as collector for its favorite interest groups. Any sort of subsidy effectively lets one group live off the resources of others and thus tends to set one domestic group against another. In World War II the Swiss government felt compelled to subsidize sales to both sides on behalf of different domestic interest groups. The balancing act was successful, but the country paid a heavy price in political disaffection.

Money, or rather the prospect of getting hold of it easily at others' expense, is the driving force of interest-group politics as well as of rapacious war. Montesquieu reminds us that the Roman Republic died when its citizens began to exploit one another as they had despoiled foreigners. This happens all too easily without pressure from foreign powers. But when a country is confronted by a foreign power that can cause rewards to flow to its favorite domestic interest groups, maintaining cohesion becomes even more difficult.

The grand question in Switzerland during World War II was whether and to what extent to resist Nazi Germany. No dispassionate person argued that this was primarily, let alone exclusively, an economic question. And yet much of the interplay among Swiss elites went on as if this grand, long-term question were about which interest group would get what in the short term. Do not confuse this effect of interest-group politics with democracy. Typically, interest groups exercise influence behind closed doors, while the public nature of democratic competition pushes political competitors to frame their claims at least in the language of common interest, if not the common good. Rather, Americans should be mindful that questions of material advantage are inherently divisive and distract from the proper concerns of foreign policy. Americans should be especially wary of such divisions and distractions because in the 1990s the United States adopted the long-standing European and Japanese theory that the purpose of foreign policy is to secure advantages for domestic businesses. Thus an official of the Clinton administration was quoted lumping all that does not concern commercial advantage into the category "Stratocrap and Globaloney."[2] No. The hunt for material advantage on the part of interest groups can corrupt foreign policy no less disastrously than domestic policy. The anti–Swiss campaign of the 1990s is yet one more example that domestic and international corruption are made of the same stuff.

Democracy

Democracy is just because those who bear the consequences of policy also choose it. But democracy is good also because it tends to produce policies more thoroughly thought out than those merely chosen by officials. The Swiss experience in World War II teaches that people at large often have a better sense of events than do their officials. This is not to say that rank–and–file citizens are intellectually brighter than elites; intelligence is not the point. Nor is *vox populi* to be confused with *vox Dei* because greater numbers lead to better decisions. History is full of instances in which whole peoples made disastrous decisions after full deliberation. None is more poignant than the ancient Athenian assembly's self–destructive decision to invade Sicily after rejecting the better arguments. Rather, popular government, or the responsibility of officials to voters, only raises the chances that the better arguments will be considered along with the worse.

Indeed, quite apart from democracy, merely adhering to formal procedures in decision-making forces officials to explain what they are doing to one another and *a fortiori* to themselves. Officials must then formulate their proposals in full sentences, knowing that they will be held responsible. As we have seen, the Swiss government likely would not have made the errors it did with regard to refugee policy and freedom of the press had the decisions been made through the normal political process, never mind by referendum. The political will to resist Nazi Germany and assert the old Swiss decencies resided far more in ordinary people than in sophisticates.

This is a valuable lesson. Americans at the turn of the century as during the Cold War have been seduced by the argument that their historically unsubtle approach to international affairs—especially revulsion at Communist regimes and preference for using military power decisively or not at all—is dangerously unsophisticated. These matters, so goes the new wisdom, are best left to the pros. One of the clearest articulations of this point comes in the 1995 memoirs of General Colin Powell (U.S. Army, retired), former national security adviser and chairman of the Joint Chiefs of Staff. Powell, proud of his status as a Washington insider, argues not only that the people's elected representatives are a bother to serious policy-makers because they play to the public, but also that seriousness in policy-making consists of privately brokering the interests of various bureaucracies and interest groups. Powell has contempt for those officials who try to make policy by presenting full-dress arguments in "big meetings with the boss." Competent men like himself instead arrange small meetings where different interests are arbitraged without the participants having to fear being held responsible. Alas, officials who make decisions *en canaille* tend to lose the intellectual discipline and the very language of national interest that are the currency of "big meetings with the boss."

What would General Guisan have said to that? In the dark years of 1940–1943 the main threat to his country's survival and to his soldiers' capacity to fight came precisely from the pros. If the Swiss elites had merely arbitraged their interests, Switzerland would have capitulated to the Nazis behind the backs of the soldiers. So this Swiss general made sure that arguments for resisting the Nazis got wide distribution among the people, and that members of parliament were fully aware of all the ways in which the Federal Council was failing to back the army. His Army and Hearth organization also helped rouse public opinion against any notion of tolerating pro-Nazi activities that might have crossed official minds. The Federal Council resented the army's political role, not least because it just did not want the issues of the war debated in public. The council members preferred not to discuss their views publicly because they believed that the people would not understand and should obey out of respect for the offices they held. But the power of office depends on legitimacy, and an official earns legitimacy by embodying a people's hopes and pride. By acting precisely as Powell advises, the Swiss federal government lost not only the argument over policy, but legitimacy as well.

Latter-Day U.S. Foreign Policy

The anti-Swiss campaign of 1995–1998 shows that America's role in the world is being undermined by unseriousness—about the realities of international affairs, brought on by a kind of corruption.

It is little wonder that at the end of the twentieth century an important contributor to America's ruling party was able to enlist the president and enough officials of that party to help extort a large sum from foreign companies doing business in the United States through a trial-less class action suit. Nor was the amount of money involved intolerable; the 10 percent of profits that the Swiss banks had to pay was roughly comparable to what foreign companies in Mexico have to pay as the "*mordida*," the local bribe. In our time, exchanging favors for permits is the way political business is done in America as well. Yet it is remarkable how quickly the practitioners of this low art went from extracting money from American companies on the basis of fraudulent claims about the harmfulness of products to attacking a whole foreign country based on imputed guilt for one of history's greatest crimes and in the sacred name of its victims.

More interesting than the corruption and chutzpah themselves are the reasons why U.S. officials felt safe in them. As often happens in history's rare prolonged periods of peace, the prospect of war becomes difficult to take seriously. To consider international affairs without war engenders behavior as unrealistic as might follow from considering relations between men and women while abstracting from intercourse and children. And so U.S. officials play at international relations mindless of the realities. It can be fun to wield the country's tremendous power unofficially, without actually committing the nation to anything, without ever putting anything to a vote. It also can be quite a bit safer to take on weak foreign countries than powerful domestic rivals. After all, the United States is so powerful that modern Germany, never mind Switzerland, can do little harm to us. So why not satisfy a valued contributor at the expense of Swiss or German companies? And why not do it in the name of moral principle?

Why not? First, because the fraudulent use of moral principle is immoral and the cynicism it engenders drives legitimate moral concerns even further out of international life. That is especially significant for America, whose relations with the rest of the world have rested to an unusual degree on claims to moral principle. It was unusually galling that the Clinton administration extorted money from Switzerland and other

European countries based on gratuitous accusations of responsibility for the Holocaust. By themselves such insults, much less the injuries, would not ruin American foreign policy. But the unseriousness of which they are part may well do so.

Second, any nation's international power is based to some extent on the admiration and awe it engenders in other nations. Nowadays that is called "soft power." In the half century after U.S. soldiers earned it by hard sacrifice in World War II, America's soft power in Europe—and in much of the world—was overwhelming. Whatever else foreigners might have thought, they believed that America was imitable, was not out to hurt them, and knew how to get its way. The Soviet Union's calls for anti-Americanism fell mostly on deaf ears; anti-Americanism was confined to the fever swamps of leftist intellectuals. But beginning in the mid-1990s, when Russian and Chinese diplomats shopped around the world the argument that decadent America was dealing high-handedly with everyone, and that everyone should oppose American hegemony, more and more people outside Paris's Left Bank listened. As the twentieth century came to an end, opinion polls throughout Europe showed that between 60 percent and 70 percent of respondents thought the United States was unfriendly to their interests and should not be imitated. In other parts of the world, resentment of America was even more prominent.

Why? Consider, first, how latter-day American popular culture is sweeping the world. It is difficult to argue that the images we are exporting—rap music, public scandal—are anything but corrosive of any and all cultures. But in the political realm, consider how difficult it is for friends of the United States to deny charges that America's claims of impartial, uncorrupt government are hypocritical. After all, U.S. administrations,

Republican and Democrat alike, long ago acquired the habit of using official power to further the commercial interest of their constituents. The Clinton administration has often reserved seats on international trade delegations for political supporters—just as its Republican predecessors did before. Other governments do so routinely, but again, when mighty, self-righteous America does it, everyone notices and resents it.

Foreign policy is supposed to project power, both soft and hard. Whatever a country lacks in the capacity to make foreigners tremble it must make up in the capacity to attract them, and vice versa. But a prerequisite for awing or attracting is a foreign policy whose voice the whole country will support morally and physically. Yet almost by definition a foreign policy that is no more than what former Secretary of Defense James Schlesinger called the stapling together of the goals of domestic constituency groups is more likely to invite all manner of disrespect.

Regardless of whether military power is used or only brandished, the military operations had better be of the same order of magnitude as the political objectives. In the aftermath of the 1991 Gulf War the United States demanded that Iraq stop manufacturing weapons of mass destruction; in the 1999 Yugoslav war the Americans insisted that Yugoslav President Slobodan Milosevic stop chasing non-Serbs out of various parts of his country. Since meeting these demands would have meant death to the regimes of both countries, they would never bend to any but mortal military operations. Moreover, these regimes realized that the United States was not about to use its full power to unseat them. So they fought. To gain its objectives, the United States would have had to use *force majeure*. But it used *force mineure*, and lost its objectives.

All this would matter little if the United States were something like a fortress—if, like republican Rome prior to the Third Punic War, its military strength and ferocity increased dramatically the closer one got to it, and its national unity were unshakable. But at the dawn of the twenty-first century America's military forces were spread over the globe as never before, and were more dependent than ever on the goodwill of allies. And more than ever, America's foreign affairs either were of no interest to the American people or were bones of interest-group contention. When the U.S. government takes part in quarrels abroad that do not energize the American people as a whole, it drains the reservoir or public spiritedness. Hence it is no small thing whenever the U.S. government foments abroad disaffection with America—especially when U.S. military power is shrinking and America continually displays international ineffectiveness. In the 1990s the image of imperiousness, moral hypocrisy, and impotence was becoming ever more dangerous to America.

One of the lessons of the Swiss experience in World War II, and indeed of any nation's experience in any serious matter, is that military power—the capacity and willingness to destroy or to protect—is the foundation of international relations. The outstanding fact about America in the 1990s, and especially during the Clinton administration, was that, even as American military forces were being spread from the Persian Gulf to Haiti to the Balkan peninsula, their size shrank by some 45 percent. At the same time the U.S. government was making military threats and promises it could not possibly keep, such as protecting the eastern borders of Poland, Hungary, and the Czech Republic, and possibly of Ukraine. As regards the Balkans, President Clinton called "immoral" the Vance-Owen plan to give the Serbs as much as 43 percent of Bosnia, and then bombed to obtain an agreement that gave them 49 percent. The United States raged against North Korea's and Iran's development of nuclear weapons and long-range missiles, and then watched as these programs moved to fruition. America bombed Iraq to force it to accept United Nations inspections of its weapons of mass destruction, and then, as Iraq continued to build what its dictator wished, the United States agreed to increase his income from oil sales, making sanctions a joke and accepting the absence of arms inspectors. Moreover, the chief targets of U.S. military power, Saddam Hussein and Slobodan Milosevic, had survived and their influence in their regions had increased while that of the United States had waned. Obviously, more and more of the world's people had less and less to hope and fear from "hard" U.S. military power.

More important, during the 1990s the world noticed a new qualitative aspect of American military power, namely that U.S. military operations were being designed less to achieve military results than to hold U.S. casualties to zero. Of course, military threats and promises conditioned on zero expenditure of lives can neither eliminate enemies nor safeguard friends. In other words they are not for real. So why would one engage in such operations? What purpose do they serve? Alas, American military operations must stress avoidance of casualties above effectiveness precisely because foreign policies franchised to interest groups cannot give the American people sufficient reason to commit their blood. They serve no purpose for the country as a whole, but rather succeed in making politicians look good to their favorite domestic constituents. In the end, they prove to be shows put on at the expense of the national interest.

As for soft power, little constituency services such as those the U.S. Democratic Party performed for Edgar Bronfman and the World Jewish Congress taught a destructive lesson: the U.S. government's talk of righteousness is less a banner that the American people can follow than a fig leaf for special interests.

What, then, can be said of a foreign policy that insults a lot and injures a little, that advertises its impotence by speaking loudly while whittling down its military stick? Quite simply that it teaches its people the wrong lessons, and that American policy-makers themselves are in need of many lessons. May God administer them gently.

Notes

Preface

[1] According to the Federal Election Commission, Edgar Bronfman donated $595,000 to the Democratic National Committee during the 1995–1996 election cycle. During that cycle Bronfman family members gave a total of $1,262,000, placing the family first among all Democratic personal donors.

[2] David C. Hendrickson, "The Recovery of Internationalism," *Foreign Affairs*, September–October 1994, p. 26.

[3] Samuel P. Huntington, "The Erosion of American National Interests," *Foreign Affairs*, September–October 1997, p. 49.

[4] Jane Perlez, "Conflict in the Balkans: Serbian Strategy," *New York Times*, March 29, 1999, p. A1.

Chapter 1

[1] Daniel Boorstin, *The Image: A Guide to the Pseudo Event in America* (New York: Harper & Row, 1964).

[2] Hearings before the U.S. Senate Committee on Banking, Housing, and Urban Affairs, May 14, 1997.

[3] Hearings before the U.S. Senate Committee on Banking, Housing, and Urban Affairs, April 23, 1996. Note that in 1951 Senator Joseph McCarthy began his campaign of defamation with a speech in Wheeling, West Virginia, in which he claimed: "I have in my hand a list. . . ." The less the senator has to go on, the more he needs the pretense that he has documentary proof of something new. D'Amato, like McCarthy, had nothing new.

[4] Hearings before the U.S. Senate Committee on Banking, Housing, and Urban Affairs, April 23, 1996.

[5] See Alexander Hamilton's memorandum on the 1790 Nootka crisis. *The Papers of Alexander Hamilton,* vol. 7, Harold C. Synett, ed. (New York:

Columbia University Press, 1961), pp. 36–57. The technique of inspiring stories and then citing them as evidence for one's claim to get further press attention is fundamental to pseudo events.

⁶ How much proof of ownership should be required to gain access to a bank account is everywhere determined by law. Swiss laws on the subject are among the most restrictive in the world. These laws have caused difficulties for people who possessed far more information than Mrs. Beer did. See the case of Estelle Sapir, in "Big Swiss Bank Settles with Daughter of Nazi Victim," *New York Times*, May 5, 1998, p. A31.

⁷ Hearings before the U.S. Senate Committee on Banking, Housing, and Urban Affairs, April 23, 1996.

⁸ Hearings before the U.S. Senate Committee on Banking, Housing, and Urban Affairs, May 15, 1997.

⁹ "U.S. and Allied Efforts to Recover and Restore Gold and Other Assets Stolen or Hidden by Germany During World War II," preliminary study coordinated by Stuart E. Eizenstat, Washington, D.C., U.S. Department of State, May 1997, p. iv.

¹⁰ *Ibid.*, vi.

¹¹ *Ibid.*, viii–ix.

¹² See, for example, Peter T. White and Steve Raymer, "A Little Humanity: The International Committee of the Red Cross," *National Geographic*, November 1986. See also William H. Nicholas and Willard Culver, "Switzerland Guards the Roof of Europe," *National Geographic*, August 1950.

¹³ Hearings before the U.S. Senate Committee on Banking, Housing, and Urban Affairs, April 23, 1996.

¹⁴ Niccolò Machiavelli, *The Prince*, translated and edited by Angelo M. Codevilla (New Haven: Yale University Press, 1997), pp. 46–47.

¹⁵ See J. Murray Luck, ed., *Modern Switzerland* (Palo Alto, CA: Society for the Promotion of Science and Scholarship, 1978). See also Rolf Kieser and Kurt R. Spillman, eds., *The New Switzerland: Problems and Policies* (Palo Alto, CA: Society for the Promotion of Science and Scholarship, 1996).

¹⁶ Of the many tributes to Churchill's statesmanship, none is more instructive than the one delivered by Professor Leo Strauss on the occasion of Sir Winston's death. "The tyrant stood at the height of his power. None dared defy him." Professor Strauss's point was that Churchill showed who he was in the summer of 1940 by defying Hitler when the *führer* was most powerful. Those who sport anti-Nazism a half century after Hitler's death are in a category different from Churchill's.

¹⁷ One can get a hint of how the overwhelming majority of democratic statesmen would have behaved had Nazi victories continued from Robert Harris's novel *Fatherland* (New York: Random House, 1992).

[18] Winston Churchill, *The Second World War* (New York: Houghton Mifflin, 1948), vol. VI, p. 616.

[19] David L. Gordon and Royden Dangerfield, *The Hidden Weapon: The Story of Economic Warfare* (New York: Harper, 1947), p. 75.

[20] Amos Elon, "Switzerland's Lasting Demon," *New York Times Magazine*, April 12, 1998, p. 43.

[21] *Une Suisse Sans Armée* (Zurich), especially #26, Summer 1995.

[22] See J. Fink, *Die Schweitz aus der Sicht des Dritten Reiches 1933–1945* (Zurich, 1985) and H.R. Kurz, *Operationsplannung Schweitz* (Thoune, 1974).

[23] Alexander Hamilton, "Pacificus No. III," *The Papers of Alexander Hamilton*, vol. 15.

[24] Note the classic refutation of the vulgar notion that "money is the sinew of war" in Niccolò Machiavelli, *Discourses*, Book II, Chapter 10. In essence Machiavelli teaches that power makes money, not the other way around.

Chapter 2

[1] Niccolò Machiavelli, *Discourses*, Book II, Ch. 27. Machiavelli illustrates the consequences of putting one's country wholly at the mercy of an aroused, victorious enemy. In particular, Machiavelli recalls the strategic error of the Florentine Republic in 1512. Even though the much superior Spanish army had offered Florence the chance to retain its republican form of government in exchange for concessions, Florence chose to fight, using the small army that Machiavelli himself had organized. Florence lost, the republic died, and Machiavelli spent the next six months in jail. His advice here is much like that of a good attorney: measure your case and then settle!

[2] Kurt von Schuschnigg, *The Brutal Takeover* (New York: Atheneum, 1971).

[3] Hans Ulrich Jost, *Nouvelle Histoire de la Suisse et des Suisses* (Lausanne, 1974), p. 157.

[4] See Edgar Bonjour, *Histoire de la Neutralité Suisse*, vols. IV, VI (Neuchatel, 1970); Daniel Bourgeois, *Le Troisième Reich et la Suisse* (Neuchatel, 1974); Jon Kimche, *Spying for Peace: General Guisan and Swiss Neutrality* (London: Weidenfeld and Nicolson, 1961).

[5] General Henri Guisan, *Rapport du General Guisan à l'Assemblée Fédérale Sur le Service Actif 1939–1945* (Bern, 1946), p. 5.

[6] Quoted in E. Bucher, "Die Schweitz im Sommer 1940," *Revue Suisse d'Histoire*, 1979, pp. 356–398.

[7] Quoted in Philippe Marguerat, *La Suisse Face au IIIème Reich* (Lausanne, 1991), p. 59.

[8] Adriano Pennacini, ed., *Cesare Opera Omnia* (Turin, Paris: Einaudi, Gallimard Pleiade, 1993); *De Bellum Galiae*, Book I, Ch. 1, p. 6.

[9] Niccolò Machiavelli, *The Prince*, Angelo Codevilla, ed. (New Haven: Yale University Press, 1997), Ch. 26. In his larger work, the *Discourses*, Machiavelli qualified that praise considerably. His main military point in the *Discourses* is that no arm or mode of warfare is inherently superior to another, and that any set of means must be used according to circumstances. At any rate, in 1515 the Swiss suffered a serious defeat at the hands of the French at the Battle of Marignano. Thereafter, Swiss influence in European affairs declined. See George Soloveitchik, *Switzerland in Perspective* (London: Oxford University Press, 1954).

[10] Guisan, *Rapport*, 196.

[11] Army Order 10067, June 3, 1940.

[12] Winston Churchill, *The Second World War* (New York: Houghton Mifflin, 1949), vol. II, p. 122.

[13] W. Roesch, *Bedrohte Schweitz* (Frauenfeld, 1986); W. Roesch, "Plans d'Attaque Allemands Contre la Suisse du Second Semestre de 1940," *Supprimer l'Armée* (Frauenfeld, 1988), pp. 55–66.

[14] On Termopylae, see Herodotus. On Demosthenes' brilliant tactics at Pylos, see Thucydides, *The Peloponnesian War*, Book V.

[15] Guisan, *Rapport*, 39.

[16] Some modern Swiss writers (see, for example, Philippe Marguerat, *La Suisse Face au IIIème Reich* [Lausanne, Editions 24 Heures]) compare the Swiss decision to forsake defense for deterrence to the U.S. decision in the 1960s to leave America defenseless against nuclear weapons. They cite Thomas Schelling's *The Strategy of Conflict* (New Haven: Yale University Press, 1966) as the classic explanation of why maintaining peace depends on accepting unacceptable consequences for one's own side in case of war. But this line of argument confuses the Swiss predicament in World War II, when defense was impossible, with the U.S. situation of the 1960s, when officials rejected options for defense and chose vulnerability on purely ideological grounds.

[17] Thucydides, *The Peloponnesian War*, Book II. Thucydides was a favorite of Colonel Max Gonard, one of General Guisan's favorite thinkers.

[18] Guisan, *Rapport*, 36–40.

[19] The precise figures are found in Jakob Huber, *Rapport du Chef de l'Etat Major de l' Armée* (Bern, 1946), pp. 112–142.

[20] Guisan, *Rapport*, 87–92.

[21] *Ibid.*, 87.

[22] Huber, 251–255.

[23] *Ibid.*, 525.

24 Jost, 164.

25 Consider: "Treason doth never prosper; what's the reason? / For if it prosper, none dare call it treason" (Sir John Harrington, "Of Treason," *Epigrams*).

26 See, for example, Machiavelli, *The Prince*, Ch. 17: "When need is far away [men] offer you their blood, their goods, their lives, their children; but when need closes in, they revolt."

27 The original sources on subversion in Switzerland during the war are the reports of the Federal Council of December 26, 1945 (FF1946, I, 1), the report of the Federal Council of May 17, 1946 (FF II, 165), and the report of the Federal Council of May 21, 1946 (FII 203). These are summarized in Albert Picot, *L'Activité Antidemocratique Contre la Suisse Pendant la Guerre* (National Council, October 9, 1946). The best historical summary of the fight for public opinion in Switzerland is Andre Lasserre, *La Suisse des Années Sombres* (Lausanne, 1989).

28 The assassin, a young Jew named David Frankfurter, was released after the war and made a career in the Israeli Ministry of Defense.

29 By the same token, after listening to *Wehrmacht* General Franz Halder's description of how German armies had sliced through Poland, Swiss Army Chief of Staff Jakob Huber crushed his cheap cigar and remarked, "Here, nobody will pass." Of course this brave tone vanished after June 1940.

30 This was revealed in a parliamentary inquest after the war. See M. André Picot, *Les Menées Hitleriennes*, Séance du Conseil National du 9 Octobre 1946, Bulletin Sténographique des Chambres Fédérales (Bern, 1946), p. 4.

31 Major de Vallière, quoted in Lasserre, *La Suisse des Années Sombres*, p. 6.

32 See, for example, a speech he delivered in 1935: "They hate [the army] because it is the obstacle, the wall against which the Bolshevik wave of 1918 broke. Because to utopian dreams it opposes its fidelity, its solidarity, its spirit of brotherhood, and if necessary its force. Because of all the products of our soil it is the one with the deepest roots" (Lasserre, 36).

33 *Plan de Causerie #22* (Archive Armée et Foyer Bern, Bibliotheque Militaire Nationale).

Chapter 3

1 This theme is fully developed in Paul Seabury and Angelo Codevilla, *War Ends and Means* (New York: Basic Books, 1989), Ch. 1.

2 *Feuille Fédérale*, 1935, vol. II, p. 561. We translate correctly the phrase "under observation of the Federal Assembly and public opinion." However,

in French, Italian, and German, the words for "observe" retain an etymological but practically vestigial implication of "control." No. Public opinion and parliament retained only the right to look on, and applaud or complain.

[3] *Documents Diplomatiques Suisses*, vol. VIII, p. 349.

[4] See Andre Lasserre, *Frontières et Camps* (Lausanne: Payot, 1995), pp. 28, 29.

[5] Lasserre, *Frontières*, 42.

[6] Quoted in Lasserre, *Frontières*, 55, 56.

[7] Karl Barth, *Eine Schweitzer Stimme 1938–1945* (Zollikon, 1946).

[8] Victor Klemperer, *I Will Bear Witness: A Diary of the Nazi Years 1942–1945* (New York: Random House, 2000).

[9] Quoted in Alfred Hasler, *The Lifeboat Is Full* (New York: Funk & Wagnalls, 1969), p. 81.

[10] The authoritative account of this key episode is in Karl Ludwig, "*La Politique Pratiquée par la Suisse à l'Egard des Réfugiés au Cours des Années 1933–1955* (Bern, 1957). See also Lasserre, *Frontières*, 167–168.

[11] This is a lesson that a variety of American institutions, especially school districts and businesses, had to learn painfully in the 1990s in the wake of court decisions regarding "sexual harassment." Having recognized the principle that such an offense exists, and not having stopped any given behavior, they became liable to the charge that such behavior falls under the prohibited category and that they approved of it.

[12] Georg Kreis, *Zensur und Selbstzensur Die Schwitzerische Presspolitik im Zweiten Weltkrieg* (Stuttgart, Frauenfeld: Huber, 1973), p. 154. See also Edgar Bonjour, *Histoire de la Neutralité Suisse*, vol. V, pp. 155–191.

[13] Memorandum Rezzonico E2001 (E) 1/5 Archives Fédérales, Bern. See also Georg Kreis, *Juli 1940* (Zurich).

[14] Denis de Rougemont, "A Cette Heure où Paris. . .," *Gazette de Lausanne*, June 17, 1940.

[15] *Manifeste du Mouvement National Suisse*, September 20, 1940 (Bern, Archives Nationales).

Chapter 4

[1] "Ubersicht des Spezialhandels nach Landern 1927–1950," *OZD Schweizerische Handelsstatistik* (Bern, 1955).

[2] André Allisson, *Exportation du Matériel de Guerre 1938–1941* (Université de Neuchatel Institut d'Histoire, May 1976).

[3] Archives Fédérales Suisses, *Les Accords Germano Suisses de la Seconde Guerre Mondiale* (Bern, 1997), p. 915. See also *Historische Statistik der Schweitz*, Ritzman/Siegenthaler S,675, Jaresberichte der OZD.

[4] *Les Accords Germano Suisses de la Seconde Guerre Mondiale*, 914.

[5] Royden and Dangerfield, 81–84.

[6] Quoted in Marguerat, *La Suisse Face au IIIème Reich*, 110.

[7] Werner Rings, *L'Or des Nazis* (Lausanne: Payot, 1985), pp. 97–98.

[8] *Ibid.*, 93.

[9] Letter of Per Jacobson to Eugen Weber, president of the Swiss National Bank, November 25, 1940, quoted in K. Urner, "E Pohl und die Schweiterische Nationalbank," *Schweitzer Monatshefte*, 1985, pp. 623–631.

[10] Rings, 41–43.

[11] The balances of the major banks are quoted at some length in the *Bergier Commission Report*, Bern, 1998, pp. 158–164.

[12] *Ibid.*

[13] Union Bank of Switzerland Annual Report, 1042, p. 9, quoted in *Bergier Commission Report*, 157.

[14] Swiss National Bank archives, meeting of February 29, 1940, #164, p. 71, quoted in *Bergier Commission Report*, 64.

[15] *Bergier Commission Report*, 64–68.

[16] Quoted in *Bergier Commission Report*, 32.

[17] Thomas McKittrick, an American official of the Bank of International Settlements, estimated in 1946 that the Reichsbank's gold stock prior to the acquisition of gold from Belgium, the Netherlands, and Luxembourg amounted to 2.1 billion Swiss francs (Marguerat, 143).

[18] Gordon and Dangerfield, 169.

[19] Eizenstat report, 196.

[20] For a thorough exploration of this myth see Chapter 2 of Nicholas Faith, *Safety in Numbers* (New York: Viking, 1982).

Chapter 5

[1] See, for example, Nathaniel C. Nash, "Swiss Raise Hopes of Tracing Lost War Deposits," *New York Times*, August 3, 1995, p. A3.

[2] Edgar Bronfman, *The Making of a Jew* (New York: Putnam, 1996).

[3] *Wall Street Journal*, January 12, 2000, p. A22.

[4] Leslie Wayne, "Trial Lawyers Pour Money Into Democrats' Chests," *New York Times*, March 23, 2000, p. A1.

[5] *New York Times*, News of the Week in Review, March 25, 2000.

[6] This is the position of, among others, former Secretary of Labor Robert Reich. See "Don't Democrats Believe in Democracy?" *Wall Street Journal*, January 12, 2000, p. A22.

[7] Alan Feuer, "2 Brooklyn Lawyers Outline a Court Patronage System," *New York Times*, January 5, 2000.

[8] Stuart Eizenstat, Letter to the Editor, *Wall Street Journal,* June 5, 2000, p. A33.

[9] John Auters *et al.*, "Banks Pay a High Price for Putting the Past Behind Them," *Financial Times*, September 9, 1998, p. 4.

[10] Author's interview with Richard Capone, January 18, 1999.

[11] John J. Goldman, "Holocaust Survivors Urge OK of Bank Claim Deal," *Los Angeles Times*, November 30, 1998, p. 14.

[12] Marilyn Henry, "Swiss Holocaust Agreement Finalized…." *Jerusalem Post*, January 24, 1999, p. 4.

[13] Barry Miller, "Jewish Groups Fight Over Spoils of Swiss Case," *New York Times*, November 29, 1998, p. 1.

[14] Charles Krauthammer, "Stop the Holocaust Treasure Hunter" *Jerusalem Post*, December 7, 1998, p. 8.

[15] Volcker report, pp. 12–13.

[16] *Ibid.*, 20–21.

[17] Michael Hirsh, "What's Taking So Long?" *Newsweek*, April 13, 1998, p. 49.

[18] Goldman, 14.

[19] Among many reports on Swiss public opinion on this matter, see Bernard D. Kapolan, "Holocaust Gold Becomes Political Football," *Nando Times News*, August 16, 1997.

[20] Luzi Stamm, *Der Kniefall Der Schweitz* (Zofinger Tagblatt, 1999) and Yves Fricker *et al.*, *La Suisse Face à l'Empire Américain* (Journal de Genève, 1997).

[21] Christoph Blocher, "Switzerland and the Eizenstat Report," speech given at a function organized by the Swiss People's Party of the canton of Bern, June 21, 1997.

[22] *New York Times*, News of the Week in Review, September 13, 1998, p. 1.

[23] David E. Sanger, "Germany Approves New Plan to Pay Holocaust Victims," *New York Times*, February 10, 1999, p. A10.

[24] Edmund Andrews, "Germany Accepts $5.1 Billion Accord to End Claims of Nazi Slave Workers," *New York Times*, December 18, 1999, p. A10.

Chapter 6

[1] This idea—that America was a danger to the world, and that the defeat in Vietnam had been necessary to exorcise that danger—was precisely the thesis of a volume edited by Anthony Lake, a pillar of U.S. foreign policy in the Nixon, Carter, and Clinton administrations. In fact, the idea had become

the conventional wisdom of Lake's class by the time of President Jimmy Carter's 1977 speech at Notre Dame that the defeat in Vietnam had enabled America to rediscover its own values.

See Anthony Lake *et al.*, *The Vietnam Legacy: The War, American Society, and the Future of American Foreign Policy* (New York: New York University Press, 1976). Especially noteworthy is the chapter by Morton Halperin, "The Lessons Nixon Learned," which argues that if American anti-Communism had not been defeated in Vietnam, the United States might well have started a nuclear war.

[2] Lawrence F. Kaplan, "The Selling of American Foreign Policy," *The Weekly Standard*, April 23, 1997, pp. 19–22.

Index

Vietnam, 29, 79, 141, 205, 212
Vietnam War, 213–14
Viking Line, 72
Volcker, Paul: auditing of accounts and, 2, 197; settlement agreement and, 187
Volcker commission, 194–95, 197–98
Volkswagen, 207

Wahlen, Friedrich Traugott, 119, 120
Waldheim, Kurt, 172
Wallensee, 48
Wall Street Journal, 5
war: democracy and, 83; economic relationships and, 23; enemies and, xiv; foreign policy in, xiii; materials essential to, 129; property rights and, 159–61; realities of, ix, xv
War of 1812, 20
War Trade Agreement, 137–38, 139, 145
Washington, George, 19–20, 212
Weber, Eugen, 148
Wehrbriefe, 80
Wehrmacht, 15, 31, 33, 49, 72, 73, 81

Weibel, Max, 71, 72, 80
Weiss, Melvyn I., 191, 196, 206
Weisshaus, Gizella, 196
Weisshaus et al. v. Union Bank of Switzerland et al., 184
Wille, Ulrich, 35–36, 42, 61–62
willingness to die, 52–53
Wilson, Woodrow, 93
World Jewish Congress (WJC): anti-Swiss campaign and, 5, 174; Bronfman and, x, 173–75; campaign against Germany and, 208; class action lawsuits and, 183–84; Clinton and, 210; distribution of settlement proceeds and, 195–97, 201–2; Eisenhower administration and, 165; Holocaust reports and, 103; power of, 172, 175; reparations from Swiss government and, 1; settlement agreement and, 192; Singer and, xii; suit against Swiss banks of, 185; Swiss public opinion of, 204; Swiss reparations and, 4;

Swiss settlement with, 175
World Jewish Restitution Organization, 202
World War I: economic warfare and, 129; France and, 42; freedom of the press and, 107–8; Germans in, 14; Germany and, 42, 159–60; Switzerland in, 14, 41–43; *Überfremdung* and, 93
World War II: balance of power in, xii; context of, 3; critical period of, 52; economics and, 126, 128–29; financial settlements following, 164; hard currency and, 146–47; lessons from, ix; neutrals in, xiii

Yugoslavia, xiii–xv

Zeiss, 161
Zulus, 37
Zurich, 19, 40, 48, 54; Swiss intelligence in, 69
Zurich Lake, 48
Zurich National Exposition of 1939, 77, 94
Zymanska, Halina, 72